Medical Assistant Exam Review

Medical Assistant Test Prep

Jane John-Nwankwo RN, MSN

5/18/16
GB
$29.97

Medical Assistant Exam Review: Medical Assistant Test Prep.

Copyright © 2014 by Jane John-Nwankwo RN, MSN

ISBN-13: 978-1495435096

ISBN-10: 1495435091

Printed in the United States of America.

Dedication

Dedicated to all the workers of Best American Healthcare University.

TABLE OF CONTENTS

Test 1

1. Which of this is not a reason for the existence of medical records?
   a. Assist physician in providing the best possible medical care for the patient
   b. Provides statistical information that is helpful to researchers
   c. Vital for financial reimbursement
   d. None of the above

2. Who owns the medical record?
   a. Patient
   b. Physician
   c. Patient's sponsor
   d. Insurance Company

3. Adopting a medical record management system that works in other facilities is the best as it saves time and you are sure it will work?
   a. True
   b. False
   c. At times
   d. None of the above

4. Which of this is not a major type of patient's medical record?

a. Paper-based

b. Computer-based

c. Objective-based

d. None of the above

5. Which of the following is also called the "electronic health record"?

    a. Paper-based

    b. Computer-based

    c. Objective-based

    d. Subjective-based

6. In the organization of the medical record, which of this is seen as the traditional patient record?

    a. Problem oriented medical record

    b. SOAP

    c. Source oriented

    d. None of the above

7. Which of the following is sometimes referred to as the "weed system"?

    a. Problem oriented medical record

    b. SOAP

    c. Source oriented

    d. None of the above

8. The "S" in SOAP is an acronym for?
    a. Start
    b. Shingling
    c. Subjective
    d. Selection

9. The "O" in SOAP is an acronym for?
    a. Objection
    b. Order
    c. Oriented
    d. Objective

10. The "A" in SOAP is an acronym for?
    a. Assessment
    b. Align
    c. Adapt
    d. Alignment

11. The "P" in SOAP is an acronym for?
    a. Problem
    b. Plan
    c. Prepare
    d. Prognosis

12. Information gained by questioning the patient or taken from a form is known as?
    a. Subjective Information

b. Objective Information

c. Computer Based

d. Paper Based

13. Information that is gathered by watching or observing of a patient is?
    a. Subjective Information
    b. Objective Information
    c. Computer Based
    d. Paper Based

14. Which of this is not a subjective information?
    a. Personal Demographics
    b. Patient's family history
    c. Patient's chief complaint
    d. Diagnosis

15. The Medical Administrative Assistant should take the following steps to establish a patient's medical record except:
    a. Determine the patient's status in the office
    b. Enter the patient's name into the computerized ledger
    c. Assemble the appropriate forms, prepare the folder and file as necessary
    d. All of the Above

16. A decision made based on the information regarding the patient's history and the results of the doctor's examination is called
    a. Prognosis
    b. Diagnosis
    c. Patient's chief complaint
    d. All of the above

17. Medical record created using information like past illnesses, surgical operations, and the patient's daily health habits gathered from the patient is known as:
    a. Patient's Family History
    b. Patient's Social History
    c. Diagnosis
    d. Personal and Medical History

18. When making corrections to a medical record which of this is appropriate to do?
    a. Erase using Correction fluid
    b. Rewrite on the Error
    c. Draw a line through the error and insert the correction above
    d. All of the above

19. After all medical records has been reviewed for the day, if it is impossible to be filed before the close of day, it should be?
    a. Placed in a file tray and locked away
    b. Left on the medical assistant table as a reminder to be filed the next day
    c. Put on the Physician's table
    d. Any of the above

20 Which of this is not a filing classification of records?
    e. Open
    f. Closed
    g. Active
    h. Inactive

21. When no restriction exist for retention of medical record, it is best the record be kept for a period of?
    a. 5 months
    b. 5 years
    c. 1 year
    d. 10 years

22. When a patient decides that he or she no longer agrees to release medical information to third party, which of this form does he need to sign?

a. Non-release form

b. Retention form

c. Revocation form

d. All of the above

23. Which of this is not involved in the process of dictations and transcription?

    a. Dictating into a dictation unit

    b. Listening to what has been dictated

    c. Keyboarding dictated text to a printed document

    d. None of the above

24. Which of this is not a consideration in selecting filing equipment?

    a. Availability of office space

    b. Color of cabinet

    c. Size and volume of record

    d. Retrieval speed

25. Which of the following is the most economic but offer little protection or confidentiality to the records?

    a. Drawer files

    b. Shelf files

    c. Rotary circular files

    d. Lateral files

26. When some marks are placed on the paper indicating that it is now ready for filing is called?
   a. Bookmark
   b. File mark
   c. Releasing
   d. Ready filing

27. _____ means deciding where to file letters or paper?
   a. Coding
   b. Indexing
   c. Conditioning
   d. Releasing

28. _____ means placing some indication of the decision on where to file on the paper?
   a. Coding
   b. Indexing
   c. Conditioning
   d. Releasing

29. When storing or filing papers in the folder, items should be placed?
   a. Face down
   b. Face up

c. Top edge to the right

d. Any of the above

30. In filing, the middle name comes?

    a. Middle

    b. First

    c. Second

    d. Third

31. In filing, the last name comes?

    a. Last

    b. First

    c. Second

    d. Third

32. In filing which of the following should come second?

    a. John-Doe Smith

    b. Jason Jackson

    c. Zee Zig

    d. Peter Street

33. How should the name John-Doe Smith be filed?

    a. Doe John Smith

    b. John Doe Smith

    c. Smith, Johndoe

    d. John-Doe Smith

34. The three basic methods of filing in healthcare facilities are as follows except?
    a. Alphabetic
    b. Numeric
    c. Color coding
    d. Subject

35. Which of the following has a direct filing system?
    a. Alphabetic
    b. Numeric
    c. Color coding
    d. Subject

36. Which of the following has an indirect filing system?
    a. Alphabetic
    b. Numeric
    c. Color coding
    d. Subject

37. Which of the following filing can either be alphabetic or alphanumeric?
    a. Alphabetic
    b. Numeric
    c. Color coding

    d. Subject

38. _____ file is used for materials that have no permanent value?
    a. Transitory file
    b. Practice management file
    c. Tickler file
    d. Follow up file

39. A filing system in which materials can be located without consulting an intermediary source of reference is?
    a. Direct filing system
    b. Indirect filing system
    c. Intermediary filing system
    d. Non intermediary filing system

40. A filing system in which an intermediary source of reference must be consulted to locate specific files is?
    a. Direct filing system
    b. Indirect filing system
    c. Intermediary filing system
    d. Non intermediary filing system

41. A film bearing a photographic record on a reduced scale of printed or other graphic matter is?

a. Photographic film

b. Graphic film

c. Micro film

d. Reduce scale film

42. A folder used to provide space for the temporary filing of materials is?
    a. Temporary file
    b. Transitory folder
    c. OUTfolder
    d. OUTguide

43. A heavy guide that is used to replace a folder that has been temporarily moved from the filing space is?
    a. Temporary file
    b. Transitory folder
    c. OUTfolder
    d. OUTguide

44. A temporary diagnosis made before all test result have been received is?
    a. Provisional diagnosis
    b. Prognosis
    c. Projectional diagnosis
    d. Temporary diagnosis

45. Which of this is not one of the 9 characteristics of quality health care?
    a. Timeliness
    b. Openness
    c. Relevance
    d. Security

46. In 1996 _____ was developed to help ensure the confidentiality of medical record?
    a. HIPAA
    b. NCHS
    c. JCAHO
    d. None of the above

47. Which of the following is a nonprofit organization that assist healthcare facilities provide accreditation services?
    a. HIPAA
    b. NCHS
    c. JCAHO
    d. None of the above

48. _____ is any occurrence that could result in patient injury any type of financial loss to the healthcare facility?
    a. Carelessness
    b. Procrastination

c. Risk

d. Hazard

49. An unexpected occurrence involving death or serious physical or psychological injury or the risk thereof is?
    a. Sentinel event
    b. Unexpected event
    c. Force major
    d. Unexpected risk

50. Activities designed to increase the quality of a product or service through process or system changes that increases efficiency and effectiveness is called?
    a. Activity changes
    b. Efficiency improvement
    c. Continuous improvement
    d. Quality Assurance

51. Title II provision of the HIPAA deals with?
    a. Insurance Reform
    b. Administrative simplification
    c. Healthcare reforms
    d. Federal government laws

52. Title II provision of the HIPAA deals with?
    a. Insurance Reform
    b. Administrative simplification
    c. Healthcare reforms
    d. Federal government laws

53. Individuals or organizations that perform or assist a covered entity in the performance of a function or activity that involves the use or disclosure of individually identifiable health information is?
    a. Business associates
    b. Individual health information coverage
    c. Business health information coverage
    d. All of the above

54. A person making a complaint against a person or organisation is known as _____?
    a. Complainer
    b. Chief complaint
    c. Complainant
    d. Accuser

55. _____ is also known as due care?
    a. Divulge
    b. Appropriate care

c. Due Diligence

d. Required care

56. The effort made by an ordinary prudent or reasonable party to avoid harm to another party or himself is?

   a. Divulge

   b. Appropriate care

   c. Due Diligence

   d. Required care

57. Providers of medical or health services, individually or as organizations, that furnish, bill for or are paid for services or products is?

   a. Hospitals

   b. Health facilities

   c. Healthcare providers

   d. Medicare

58. To derive conclusion from facts and premises is called?

   a. Hypothesis

   b. Infer

   c. Concluding fact

   d. Assumption

59. The division of the federal government that enforces privacy standards is called?

a. Office of the privacy standard act
b. Office of Inspector General
c. Office for Health information Enforcement
d. Office for Civil Rights

60. The patient's own information that pertains to his or her health is called?
a. Patient's information
b. Private information
c. Personal health information
d. All of the above

61. A person designated to ensure compliance with privacy standards for a covered entity is?
a. Compliance officer
b. Submission officer
c. Privacy officer
d. All of the above

62. Transmission of information between two parties to carry out financial or administrative activies related to healthcare is?
a. Medical assistance
b. Transmissionist
c. Information transmission
d. Transactions

63. _____ is established to protect the integrity of the department of health and human services, the office conduct audits, investigation and inspection involving laws that pertains to HHS?

    a. Office of Investigation and Inspection Audit

    b. Office of Inspector General

    c. Office for Health information Enforcement

    d. Office for Civil Rights

64. When a patient has a complaint regarding his or her privacy information, the first person he should seek out is the?

    a. Office Manager

    b. Privacy officer

    c. Office for Civil Rights

    d. Office of the Inspector General

65. Which of the following must be included on a notice of privacy practices?

    a. Details of how PHI is used and disclosed by the facility

    b. Duties of providers to protect health information

c. Effective date of the notice of privacy practice

d. All of the above

66. Which of this is not a right that the patient has under privacy rule?

a. Right to request that communication from the facility be kept confidential

b. Right to charge a physician if he is not satisfied with his service

c. Right to restrict certain parts or uses of their PHI

d. Right to notice of a facility's privacy practice

67. _____ is a secondary use or disclosure that cannot reasonably be prevented, it is limited in nature and occurs as a result of another use or disclosure that is permitted?

a. Secondary Disclosure

b. Primary Disclosure

c. Permitted Disclosure

d. Incidental Disclosure

68. Services that support patient diagnoses is called?

a. Ancillary therapeutic services

b. Patient diagnoses services

c. Patient treatment services

d. Ancillary diagnostic services

69. Services that support patient treatment is called?

    a. Ancillary therapeutic services

    b. Patient diagnoses services

    c. Patient treatment services

    d. Ancillary diagnostic services

70. Converting verbal or written descriptions into numeric and alphanumeric designations is called?

    a. Filing

    b. Coding

    c. Converting

    d. Transforming

71. The determination of the nature of disease, injury, or congenital defect is?

    a. Determinant

    b. Prognosis

    c. Porosis

    d. Diagnosis

72. The acronym ICD-9-CM means?

a. International clinical data, Ninth Revision Classification Modification
b. Internal Classification of Disease Non Revised Clinical Modification
c. International Classification of Diseases Ninth Revision, Clinical Modification
d. None of the above

73. System containing the greatest number of changes in ICD history to allow specific reporting of disease and newly recognized conditions is?
    a. ICD-9-CM
    b. ICD-5-CM
    c. ICD-11-CM
    d. ICD-10-CM

74. System for classifying disease to facilitate the collection of uniform and comparable health information, for statistical purposes and indexing medical records for data storage and retrieval is called?
    a. ICD-9-CM
    b. ICD-5-CM
    c. ICD-11-CM
    d. ICD-10-CM

75. The initial identification of the condition or complaint that the patient expresses in the outpatient medical setting?
   a. Chief Complaint
   b. Initial Complaint
   c. Patient Identification
   d. Primary Diagnosis

76. The ICD-10-CM contains approximately _____ more codes that ICD-9.
   a. 5000
   b. 4500
   c. 5500
   d. 6500

77. The translation and transformation of written descriptions of diseases, illness and injury into numeric codes is called?
   a. Classification of diseases
   b. Diagnostic coding
   c. Descriptive numeric coding
   d. None of the above

78. The ICD-9-CM manuals contains three volumes, Volumes 1 & 2 are used for?
   a. Coding procedures and services performed within hospital environment
   b. V coding

c. E coding

d. Diagnostic coding

79. The ICD-9-CM manuals contains three volumes,
Volume 3 is used for?

    a. Coding procedures and services
    performed within hospital environment

    b. V coding

    c. E coding

    d. Diagnostic coding

80. Volume 1 of the ICD-9-CM manual is also
known as the?

    a. Tabular Index

    b. Numeric Index

    c. Alphabetic Index

    d. Alphanumeric Index

81. The _____ code classification is named the
supplemental classification of external causes
of injuries and poisoning?

    a. V coding

    b. A coding

    c. E coding

    d. Procedural coding

82. Volume 2 of the ICD-9-CM manual is called the?
   a. Tabular Index
   b. Numeric Index
   c. Alphabetic Index
   d. Alphanumeric Index

83. The _____ code is used on occasions when the patient is not currently ill or to explain problems that influence his current illness?
   a. V code
   b. A code
   c. E code
   d. Procedural coding

84. The _____ code is used to classify environmental causes of injury, poisoning or other adverse effect on the body?
   a. V code
   b. A code
   c. E code
   d. Procedural coding

85. The abbreviation "NOS" used on the tabular index of the ICD-9-CM means?
   a. Numbers
   b. Not on site

    c. Number of Sickness

    d. Not otherwise specified

86. The abbreviation "NEC" used on the tabular index of the ICD-9-CM means?

    a. Number of etiology classification

    b. Not excluding category

    c. Not elsewhere classifiable

    d. No external classification

87. Which of the volumes of the ICD-9-CM manual is not used in a physician's office?

    a. Volume 1

    b. Volume 2

    c. Volume 3

    d. None of the above

88. _____ is a residual problem remaining after acute phase of an illness or injury has terminated?

    a. Suspected

    b. Late effect

    c. Impending threat

    d. Parasitic Diseases

89. _____ refers to the underlying cause or origin of a disease?

    a. Manifestation

b. Etiology

c. Root cause

d. Indicators

90._____ describes the signs and
symptoms of a disease?

    a. Manifestation

    b. Etiology

    c. Root cause

    d. Indicators

91. In coding, the circulatory system section for
hypertensive disease can be found in category?

    a. 393 to 398

    b. 415 to 417

    c. 420 to 429

    d. 390 to 392

92. In coding, the circulatory system section for
acute *rheumatic fever* can be found in
category?

    a. 393 to 398

    b. 415 to 417

    c. 420 to 429

    d. 390 to 392

93. _____ is caused by a lesion on one of the coronary arteries that causes lack of blood flow to the heart?
    a. Myocardial Infarction
    b. Hypertension disease
    c. Ischemic heart disease
    d. Cerebrovascular accident

94. _____ is defined as the transformation of verbal descriptions of medical services and procedures into numeric or alphanumeric designations?
    a. Diagnostic coding
    b. Procedural coding
    c. CPT-4 manual
    d. HCPCS

95. A listing of descriptive terms and identifying codes for reporting medical services and procedures performed by physicians in order to provide a uniform or standard language that will accurately describe medical, surgical and diagnostic services and enhance reliable communication among physician is?
    a. Diagnostic coding
    b. Procedural coding
    c. CPT-4 manual
    d. HCPCS

96. Code additions that explain circumstances that alter a provided service or provide additional clarification or detail about a procedure or service is?
    a. Additional service codes
    b. Procedural code
    c. Modifiers
    d. All of the above

97. Codes in which the components of a procedure are separated and reported separately is?
    a. Subcategory code
    b. Bundled code
    c. Subsection code
    d. Unbundled code

98. Codes designating procedures or services that are grouped together and paid for as one procedure or service is?
    a. Subcategory code
    b. Bundled code
    c. Subsection code
    d. Unbundled code

99. The primary procedure or service code selected when performing insurance billing or statistical research is?
   a. Subcategory
   b. Category I code
   c. Category II code
   d. Category III code

100.   Indented one level below a category, usually a procedure or service unique to a category is?
   a. Subcategory
   b. Category I code
   c. Category II code
   d. Category III code

101.   Code for a new experimental procedure or service is called?
   a. Subcategory
   b. Category I code
   c. Category II code
   d. Category III code

102.   Special codes that can help providers track revenue and reimbursement is?
   a. Subcategory
   b. Category I code
   c. Category II code

d. Category III code

103.	A patient is diagnosed with metastatic bone neoplasm. The neoplasm will be coded as?
   a. Primary malignant
   b. Secondary malignant
   c. Carcinoma in situ
   d. Benign

104.	_____ is defined as the absence of invasion of surrounding tissues.
   a. Primary malignant
   b. Secondary malignant
   c. Carcinoma in situ
   d. Benign

105.	The _____ code is used for procedures that is always performed during the same operative session as another surgery in addition to the primary service/procedure and is never performed separately?
   a. Stand-alone codes
   b. Indented codes
   c. Add-on codes
   d. Modifiers

106. _____ is used when more than one code must be used to completely describe a specific procedure or service?
   a. Circle with a line through it
   b. Two triangular symbols
   c. A bullet
   d. A plus sign

107. _____represents a new procedure or service code added/revised since the previous edition of the CPT manual?
   a. Circle with a line through it
   b. Two triangular symbols
   c. A bullet
   d. A plus sign

108. The _____are reported as two-digit numeric codes added to the five-digit CPT code?
   a. Modifiers
   b. Add-on codes
   c. Location Method
   d. All of the above

109. All of the following are correct regarding add-on codes except:
   a. They can be reported as stand-alone codes.
   b. They are exempted from modifier-51 (multiple procedures).

c. They are performed in addition to a primary procedure.

d. The add-on procedure must be performed by the same physician

110.   What are the three key components of an E & M Code?

a. Examination, coordination of care, medical decision making

b. History, examination, medical decision making

c. History, nature of presenting problem, coordination of care

d. Nature of presenting problem, examination, coordination of care

111.   If a code is selected that not only matches the procedure or service performed but also add modifying information that is not in the medical documentation, the information is considered _____?

a. Downcoding

b. Noncoding

c. Upcoded

d. Modifying codes

112.   _____ are procedures or services named after their inventor or developer?

a. Eponyms

b. Scientist

c. Mohs

d. Crohn

113. A change in code submitted to reimbursement usually performed by the insurance company is called?

    a. Downcoding

    b. Noncoding

    c. Upcoded

    d. Modifying codes

114. Which of the following is not a category in which the E&M section is divided into?

    a. Office visits

    b. Hospital visits

    c. Consultations

    d. None of the above

115. A new patient is?

    a. One who has not visited the physician in more than 6 months

    b. One who has not been seen by any of the physicians in 3 years.

    c. Determined by the physician and staff

    d. Determined by a third-party payer

116. _____ is defined as someone who has received medical services within the last 3 years from the physician or another physician of the same specialty who belongs to the same group practice?

    a. New patient

    b. Established patient

    c. Old patient

    d. Returning patient

117. _____ is a brief statement describing the symptom, problem, diagnosis, or condition that is the reason a patient seeks medical care?

    a. Prognosis

    b. Patient medical history

    c. Chief complaint

    d. Prescription

118. Which of the following is not a circumstance under which the V codes are used?

    a. To indicate the birth status of a newborn

    b. When a circumstance may influence a patient's health status but is not a current illness or condition

c. When a person has virus that has not yet been cured

d. When a person who is not currently sick encounters the health services for some specific reason such as to act as an organ donor or receive a vaccination

119.   The _____ codes are used to describe the reason or external cause of injury?
   a. Volume 1
   b. E code
   c. V code
   d. All of the above

120.   The Abbreviation "POS" means?
   a. Position
   b. Post out of service
   c. Possible outcome solution
   d. Point of service

121.   When the patient answers questions about the eyes, ears, nose, throat and mouth it is called?
   a. Chief complaint
   b. Past medical and social history
   c. Review of systems
   d. History of present illness

122. _____ concentrates on the chief complaint, it looks at the symptoms, severity and duration of problem?
   a. Problem focused history
   b. Detailed history
   c. Expanded problem focused history
   d. Comprehensive history

123. When the physician proceeds as in the problem focused history but includes a review of the system that refers to chief complaint is?
   a. Problem focused history
   b. Detailed history
   c. Expanded problem focused history
   d. Comprehensive history

124. Which of this is not a division in examination in the evaluation and management service?
   a. Detailed examination
   b. Expanded problem focused examination
   c. Comprehensive examination
   d. None of the above

125.   In anesthesia coding, the physical status modifiers is composed of two characters, "P1" represents?
    a. A normal healthy patient
    b. A brain-dead patient whose organ are being harvested
    c. A patient with severe systemic disease
    d. A patient with mild systemic disease

126.   In anesthesia coding, the physical status modifiers is composed of two characters, "P2" represents?
    a. A normal healthy patient
    b. A brain-dead patient whose organ are being harvested
    c. A patient with severe systemic disease
    d. A patient with mild systemic disease

127.   In anesthesia coding, the physical status modifiers is composed of two characters, "P5" represents?
    a. A normal healthy patient
    b. A brain-dead patient whose organ are being harvested
    c. A patient with severe systemic disease
    d. A patient with mild systemic disease

128. _____ codes are intended to report a hydration intravenous infusion to consist of a prepackaged fluid and electrolytes but are not used to report infusion of drugs or other substance?

    a. Psychotherapy
    b. Vaccines
    c. Toxoids
    d. Hydration

129. _____ is the treatment for mental illness and behavioral disturbance in which he clinical attempts to alleviate the emotional disturbances, reverse or change maladaptive patters of behavior and encourages personality growth and development?

    a. Psychotherapy
    b. Vaccines
    c. Toxoids
    d. Hydration

130. _____ codes are reported once per month to distinguish age specific service related to the patient's end stage renal disease performed in an outpatient setting?

    a. Psychotherapy
    b. Dialysis

c. Toxoids

d. Hydration

131. _____ is an ultrasound examination of the cardiac chambers and calves, the adjacent great vessels, and the pericardium?

    a. Cardiac catheterization

    b. Echocardiography

    c. Chemotherapy

    d. Electrophysiology

132. A diagnostic medical procedure that includes introduction, positioning and repositioning of catheter, recording of intracardiac and intravascular pressure and final evaluation and reporting of the procedure is?

    a. Cardiac catheterization

    b. Echocardiography

    c. Chemotherapy

    d. Electrophysiology

133. The continuous and simultaneous monitoring and recording of various physiologic parameters of sleep for 6 or more

hours with physician review, interpretation and report is?
   a. Sleep monitoring
   b. Physiologic parameters of sleep
   c. Sleep studies
   d. All of the above

134.   An injection in which the healthcare professional who administers the substance or drugs is continuously present to administer the injection and observe the patient or an infusion of 15 minutes or less is?
   a. Intraarterial push
   b. Injection observation
   c. Acupuncture
   d. All of the above

135.   _____ procedures are performed to remove devitalized and necrotic tissue and promote healing?
   a. Acupuncture
   b. Active wound care
   c. Osteopathic Manipulative
   d. Home health procedures

136.   _____ is reported based on 15 minutes increments of personal contact with patient?

a. Acupuncture

b. Active wound care

c. Osteopathic Manipulative

d. Home health procedures

137. A form of manual treatment applied by a physician to eliminate or alleviate somatic dysfunction and related disorders is?

a. Acupuncture

b. Active wound care

c. Osteopathic Manipulative

d. Home health procedures

138. _____ codes are used by non-physician health care professionals only to report services provided in a patient's residence?

a. Acupuncture

b. Active wound care

c. Osteopathic Manipulative

d. Home health procedures

139. Which of this is not a main section of the CPT-4?

a. Surgery

b. Radiology

c. Medicine

d. None of the above

140. Which of the following is a purpose of the CPT-4?
   a. To encourage the use of standard terms and descriptors to document procedures
   b. To provide basis for a computer oriented system to evaluate operative procedures
   c. To contribute basic information for statistical purposes
   d. All of the above

141. The maximum amount of money that many third-party payors allow for a specific procedure or service is called?
   a. Maximum charge
   b. Third-party charge
   c. Allowed charge
   d. Authorized charge

142. Individual entitled to receive benefits from an insurance policy or government entitlement program offering healthcare benefits is?
   a. Beneficiary
   b. Benefiting participant
   c. Individual benefit

d. Recipient

143. Payment method used by many managed care organization wherein a fixed amount of money is reimbursed to the provider for patients enrolled during a specific period of time is?
   a. Fixed payment
   b. Enrollment reimbursement
   c. Payment reimbursement
   d. Capitation

144. Health benefits program run by the department of veterans affairs that helps eligible beneficiaries pay the cost of specific healthcare services and supplies is?
   a. CHAMPUS
   b. CHUMPVA
   c. CHAMPVA
   d. Benefits for veteran affairs

145. A policy provision frequently found in medical insurance whereby the policyholder and the insurance company share the cost of covered losses in a specified ratio is?
   a. Copayment
   b. Co-insurance

c. Co-ratio

d. Commercial insurance

146.   A sum of money that is paid at the time of medical service is?

    a. Copayment

    b. Co-insurance

    c. Co-ratio

    d. Commercial insurance

147.   Plans that reimburse the insured for expenses resulting from illness or injury according to a specific fee schedule as outlined in the insurance policy on a fee-for-service basis is?

    a. Copayment

    b. Co-insurance

    c. Co-ratio

    d. Commercial insurance

148.   Which of the following is also called subscriber?

    a. Beneficiary

    b. Benefiting participant

    c. Individual benefit

    d. Recipient

149. Which of this is sometimes called private insurance?
   a. Copayment
   b. Co-insurance
   c. Co-ratio
   d. Commercial insurance

150. Specific amounts of money a patient must pay out of pocket before the insurance carrier begins paying is?
   a. Copayment
   b. Out of pocket payment
   c. Initial payment
   d. Deductibles

151. The spouse, children and sometimes partner or other individuals designated by the insured who are covered under a healthcare plan is?
   a. Dependent
   b. Defendant
   c. Respondent
   d. Independent

152. Insurance that provides periodic payment to replace income when an insured

person is unable to work as a result of illness, injury or disease is?

    a. Employment disability

    b. Disability income insurance

    c. Illness Insurance

    d. All of the above

153.   A letter or statement from the insurance carrier describing what was paid, denied or reduced in payment is?

    a. Exclusion

    b. Explanation of benefit

    c. Explanation of Medicare Benefits

    d. Statement of Insurance

154.   Limitations on an insurance contract for which benefits are not payable is?

    a. Exclusion

    b. Explanation of benefit

    c. Explanation of Medicare Benefits

    d. Insurance limitation

155.   An established schedule of fees set for services performed by providers and paid by the patient?

    a. Scheduled fee

    b. Service performance fee

    c. Fee for service

d. All of the above

156. An organization that contracts with government to handle and dedicate insurance claims from medical facilities or providers of medical services or supplies is?
   a. Government medical organization
   b. Insurance organization
   c. Fiscal intermediary
   d. None of the above

157. The person responsible for paying a medical bill is called?
   a. Health insurance
   b. Guarantor
   c. Sponsor
   d. Medicare

158. _____ is a federal program administered by state governments to provide medical assistance to the needy?
   a. Medigap
   b. Advance Beneficiary
   c. Medicaid
   d. Medi-cal

159. _____ is a private insurance designed to help pay for those amounts that are typically the patient's responsibility under Medicare?

    a. Medigap

    b. Advance Beneficiary

    c. Medicaid

    d. Medi-cal

160. Protection against financial losses resulting from illness or injury?

    a. Financial insurance

    b. Health insurance

    c. Insurance protection

    d. All of the above

161. The periodic payment of a specific sum of money to an insurance company for which the insurer agrees to provide certain benefit is?

    a. Monthly payment

    b. Annual payment

    c. Quarterly payment

    d. Premium

162. Which of this is not a type of health insurance?

    a. Group insurance

b. Individual insurance

c. Medical savings account

d. None of the above

163. _____is a contract between a policyholder and an insurance carrier or a government program developed to reimburse the policyholder of all or most medical expenses?

a. Policy Holder contract

b. Insurance carrier contract

c. Health insurance

d. Medicare

164. Which of this is not a way an individual can obtain health insurance?

a. Group Insurance

b. Personal Insurance

c. Pre-paid Health Plan

d. Employee Insurance

165. When a group of employees and their dependents are insured under one (1) group policy issued to the employer it is called?

a. Group Insurance

b. Personal Insurance

c. Pre-paid Health Plan

d. Employee Insurance

166.   The _____ is also known
as a fee for service?
- a. Indemnity Insurance
- b. Managed Care Plans
- c. Preferred Provider Organization
- d. Point-of-Service plan

167.   _____ is a managed care plan
that gives beneficiaries the option of whom to
see for services?
- a. Preferred Provider Plan
- b. Managed Care Plans
- c. Preferred Provider Organization
- d. Point-of-Service plan

168.   The type of plan where a patient may
have where they can see providers outside
their plan is known as?
- a. Preferred Provider Plan
- b. Managed Care Plans
- c. Preferred Provider Organization
- d. Point-of-Service plan

169.   What method is used mostly in
reference to fee for-service reimbursement?

a. Relative Value Payment Schedules Method
b. Medicare's Resource Based Relative Value Scale (RBRVS) Payment Schedule
c. The Usual, Customary, and Reasonable
d. Contracted Rate Method

170. _____ Involves the use of relative value scales which assign a relative weight to individual services according to the basis for the scale?
a. Relative Value Payment Schedules Method
b. Medicare's Resource Based Relative Value Scale (RBRVS) Payment Schedule
c. The Usual, Customary, and Reasonable
d. Contracted Rate Method

171. Which of this does the Physicians agree to provide services at a discount of their usual fee in return for a pool of existing patients?
a. Contracted Rate with MCO
b. Capitated Rates
c. The Usual, Customary, and Reasonable
d. Relative Value Payment Schedules Method

172. Medicare is available for the following categories of people except?

a. Person who does not want to pay medical bill
b. persons 65 years or older, retired on Social Security benefits
c. those diagnosed with end-stage renal disease
d. spouse of a person paying into the Social Security system

173. _____is a document provided to a Medicare beneficiary by a provider prior to service being rendered letting the beneficiary know of his/her responsibility to pay if Medicare denies the claim?
a. Medigap
b. Advance Beneficiary
c. Medicaid
d. Medi-cal

174. Which of this is not a service offered by Medicaid?
a. Outpatient hospital services
b. Cosmetic procedures necessitated by an injury
c. Family planning and supplies
d. None of the above

175. _____ is a state-required insurance plan, the coverage of which provides benefits to employees and their dependents for work related injury, illness or death?

a. Employee Insurance
b. Employer Insurance
c. Workers Compensation
d. State Insurance

176. _____ is a policy that covers losses to a third party caused by the insured, by an object owned by the insured, or on premises owned by the insured?
a. Disability
b. Liability
c. Comprehensive
d. Auto insurance

177. Which of this is not a type of plan covered under the TRICARE program
a. Standard
b. Active
c. Extra
d. Prime

178. Which of the plans covered under TRICARE does not have annual deductible?
a. Standard
b. Active
c. Extra
d. Prime

179. Which of the plans covered under TRICARE is a health maintenance organization plan with a point-of-service option?

a. Standard
b. Active
c. Extra
d. Prime

180.   Which of this was created to provide medical benefits to spouses and children of veterans with total, permanent service related disabilities or for surviving spouses and children of a veteran who died as a result of service related to disability?
a. TRICARE
b. CHAMPUS
c. CHAMPVA
d. All of the above

181.   In the Medicare suffix status chart "A" means?
a. Disabled Child
b. Widow
c. Disabled adult
d. Wage earner

182.   In the Medicare suffix status chart "D" means?
a. Disabled Child
b. Widow
c. Disabled adult
d. Wage earner

183. Which of the medicare parts is referred to as Supplementary Medical Insurance?
   a. Part A
   b. Part B
   c. Part C
   d. Part D

184. Which of the medicare parts is also called Hospital Insurance for the Aged and Disabled?
   a. Part A
   b. Part B
   c. Part C
   d. Part D

185. Amongst the terms used to describe the state of submitted forms "Dirty Claim" means?
   a. Has all required fields accurately filled out, contains no deficiencies.
   b. Contains errors or omissions
   c. Requires investigation and needs further clarification
   d. Contains complete, necessary information, but is incorrect or illogical in some way

186. Amongst the terms used to describe the state of submitted forms "Rejected Claim" means?
   a. Has all required fields accurately filled out, contains no deficiencies.
   b. Contains errors or omissions

c. Requires investigation and needs further clarification

d. Contains complete, necessary information, but is incorrect or illogical in some way

187.   Amongst the terms used to describe the state of submitted forms "Invalid Claim" means?

a. Has all required fields accurately filled out, contains no deficiencies.

b. Contains errors or omissions

c. Requires investigation and needs further clarification

d. Contains complete, necessary information, but is incorrect or illogical in some way

188.   _____ is a traditional method used by providers for submission of charges to insurance companies?

a. Paper Claim

b. Electronic Claim

c. Clearinghouse

d. Universal Claim Form

189.   _____ is an entity that receives transmissions of claims from physicians' offices, separates the claims by carriers and performs software edits on each claim to check for errors?

a. Paper Claim
b. Electronic Claim
c. Clearinghouse
d. Universal Claim Form

190.   Which of the following is not a basic billing and reimbursement steps?
a. Calculate physician charges
b. Transmit claims
c. Verify insurance
d. None of the above

191.   The transmission of claims data either electronically or manually to third party payers or clearinghouses for processing is known as?
a. Claims processing
b. Claims adjudication
c. Claims submission
d. Claim Payment

192.   _____ is when the third party payers and clearinghouses verify the information found in the submitted claims about the patient and provider?
a. Claims processing
b. Claims adjudication
c. Claims submission
d. Claim Payment

193. Any procedure or service reported on the insurance claim that is not listed in the payer's master benefit list is called?
   a. Unauthorized benefit
   b. Unlisted benefit
   c. Non-covered benefit
   d. Denied Benefit

194. A procedure or service provided without proper authorization or was not covered by a current authorization
   a. Unauthorized benefit
   b. Unlisted benefit
   c. Non-covered benefit
   d. Denied Benefit

195. _____ is when the provider agrees to accept what the insurance company approves as payment in full for the claim.
   a. Assignment of benefits.
   b. Accept assignment
   c. Insurance agreement
   d. Provider-insurance acceptance

196. A patient who receives treatment in the hospital clinic or physician's office and released within 23hrs is known as?
   a. Impatient
   b. Outpatient
   c. Hospital patient
   d. Less than a day patient

197. A patient that is admitted to the hospital with the expectation that the patient will stay for a period of 24 hours or more is called?
   a. Impatient
   b. Outpatient
   c. Hospital patient
   d. More than a day patient

198. A service performed by a physician whose opinion or advice is requested by another physician in the evaluation or treatment of a patient's illness or suspected problem is called?
   a. Advisory
   b. Consultation
   c. Counseling
   d. Conferencing

199. A claim that is missing information and is returned to the provider for correction and resubmission is called?
   a. Incorrect claim
   b. Missing claim
   c. Resubmission claim
   d. Incomplete claim

200. _____ is also called invalid claim?
   a. Incorrect claim
   b. Missing claim
   c. Resubmission claim

d. Incomplete claim

201.   Which of this is a section in which the CMS-1500 is divided into?
   a. Address of the insurance carrier
   b. Physician's information
   c. Patient Information
   d. All of the above

202.   Claims without significant errors of any type is called?
   a. Non error claim
   b. Clean claim
   c. Semi-clean claim
   d. Dirty claim

203.   Inaccurate or incomplete insurance claim returned for information and correction is?
   a. Correct claim
   b. Inaccurate claim
   c. Dingy claim
   d. Partial claim

204.   _____ is referred to as the path left by electronic transaction when it has been completed?
   a. Completed trail
   b. Audit trail
   c. Tickler trail
   d. None of the above

205. A record of the charges and payment posted on an account is called?
   a. Accounts receivable ledger
   b. Account balance
   c. Account record
   d. Payment record

206. An entry on an account constituting an addition to a revenue, net worth or liability account is?
   a. Debit
   b. Credit
   c. Liability
   d. Revenue

207. An entry on an account constituting an addition to an expense or asset account or a deduction from a revenue, a net worth, or a liability account is?
   a. Debit
   b. Credit
   c. Liability
   d. Revenue

208. Funds paid out is called?
   a. Disbursement
   b. Reimbursement
   c. Repay
   d. Refund

209. An organization under contract to the government as well as some private plans to act as financial representatives in handling insurance claims from providers of healthcare is called?
   a. Financial representatives
   b. Insurance provider
   c. Fiscal agent
   d. Government financial agent

210. _____ is also referred to as fiscal intermediary?
   a. Financial representatives
   b. Insurance provider
   c. Fiscal agent
   d. Government financial agent

211. _____ is also called a write-it-once system?
   a. Posting
   b. Pegboard system
   c. Payables
   d. Premium

212. _____ is the consideration paid for a contract of insurance?
   a. Posting
   b. Pegboard system
   c. Payables
   d. Premium

213. A superiority or excess in number of quantity is?
   a. Preponderance
   b. Superior quantity
   c. Excess quantity
   d. None of the above

214. Amount paid on patient accounts is?
   a. Receivables
   b. Payment
   c. Receipts
   d. Third-party payor

215. Total monies received on account is?
   a. Receivables
   b. Payment
   c. Receipts
   d. Third-party payor

216. A method of accurately tracking patient accounts that allows the figure to be proved accurate through mathematic formulas is?
   a. Posting
   b. Pegboard system
   c. Payables
   d. Audit Trail

217. Most insurance plans base their payment of UCR fees, the "U" here means?
   a. Unilateral
   b. Union

c. Usual

d. Under

218. Most insurance plans base their payment of UCR fees, the "R" here means?
   a. Rights
   b. Reliance
   c. Reliable
   d. Reasonable

219. The slips that are attached to charts while the patient is in the office, usually for billing purpose is called?
   a. Billing slip
   b. In office slip
   c. Chart slip
   d. Encounter forms

220. When a patient has paid in advance or there has been an overpayment or duplicate payment it is called?
   a. Overpayment
   b. Debit balances
   c. Credit balances
   d. Advanced payment

221. Which of this is not a type of check?
   a. Certified check
   b. Limited check
   c. Money Order
   d. None of the above

222. Network of banks that exchange checks with one another is called?
   a. Banks exchange
   b. Check exchange
   c. Clearinghouses
   d. None of the above

223. When a mistake or an error is made on a check what should you do?
   a. Cross it out
   b. Rewrite on the error
   c. Write the word void on the check
   d. All of the above

224. Which of this is not a type of endorsement?
   a. Blank endorsement
   b. Limited endorsement
   c. Special endorsement
   d. Qualified endorsement

225. Which of this type of endorsement does the payee signs his name and makes the check payable to the bearer?
   a. Blank endorsement
   b. Limited endorsement
   c. Special endorsement
   d. Qualified endorsement

226. A person who signs his name on the back of a check for the purpose of transferring title to another person is called?

a. Imposer
b. Endorser
c. Indorser
d. Transfer of check

227. The process of providing that a bank statement and checkbook balance are in agreement is called?

a. Reconciliation
b. Balancing
c. Check bank balancing
d. All of the above

228. The method of accounting in which income is recorded when earned and expenses are recorded when incurred is?

a. Balance sheet
b. Account receivable
c. Accrual basis of accounting
d. Trial balance

229. A method of checking the accuracy of accounts is?

a. Balance sheet
b. Account receivable
c. Accrual basis of accounting
d. Trial balance

230. A financial statement for a specific date that shows the total assets, liabilities and capital of the business is called?
   a. Balance sheet
   b. Cash flow statement
   c. Statement of income and expense
   d. Disbursement Journal

231. A financial summary for a specific period that shows the beginning balance on hand, the receipts and disbursements during the period and the balance on hand at the end of the period is called?
   a. Balance sheet
   b. Cash flow statement
   c. Statement of income and expense
   d. Disbursement Journal

232. A summary of accounts paid out is called?
   a. Accounts payable
   b. Cash flow statement
   c. Statement of income and expense
   d. Disbursement Journal

233. Which of the following is not a kind of financial record?
   a. Daily Journal
   b. Checkbook
   c. Income slip
   d. Petty cash record

234. _____ is the oldest and simplest book keeping system?
    a. Double-Entry
    b. Single-Entry
    c. Write-it-once system
    d. Pegboard system

235. Which of this is not a function of a medical office manager?
    a. Recruiting new employees
    b. Planning staff meetings
    c. Dismissing employees
    d. None of the above

236. Which of this is not a type of leader?
    a. Transactional
    b. Transnational
    c. Transformational
    d. Charismatic

237. _____ leader is innovative and able to bring about change in an organization?
    a. Transactional
    b. Transnational
    c. Transformational
    d. Charismatic

238. _____ is the ability to influence employees so that they carry out their directives?
    a. Influence

b. Skill

c. Power

d. Affluence

239. _____ is a tool designed to inform employees about the duties they are expected to perform?
   a. Employee Handbook
   b. Employee manual
   c. Job description
   d. Policy manual

240. A series of executive position in order of authority is?
   a. Executive position
   b. Chain of command
   c. Organizational structure
   d. Line of management

241. The process or technique of promoting, selling and distributing a product or service is called?
   a. Promotion
   b. Marketing
   c. Outreach
   d. Target Market

242. The process of using marketing and education strategies to reach and involve diverse audiences through the use of key messages and effective programs is?
   a. Promotion

b. Marketing

c. Outreach

d. Target Market

243. A special group of individuals towards whom the marketing plan is focused is?
   a. Promotion
   b. Marketing
   c. Outreach
   d. Representing

244. Which of the following is not one of the 4 "p's" of marketing?
   a. Product
   b. Price
   c. Placement
   d. Plan

245. An accounting period of 12 months is?
   a. Annual year
   b. Fiscal year
   c. 1 year
   d. None of the above

246. Traditional health insurance plans that pay for all or a share of the cost of covered services, regardless of which physician, hospital or other healthcare provider is used is called?
   a. Indemnity
   b. Service benefit plan
   c. UCR Fee

d. Resource-based relative value scale

247. Which of this is not a health care provider?
    a. Managed care plans
    b. Blue Cross
    c. Commercial insurance
    d. None of the above

248. Which of this is not a model of managed care?
    a. HMO
    b. PPO
    c. MCO
    d. None of the above

249. A fee schedule designed to provide national uniform payment of medicare benefits after being adjusted to reflect the differences in practice cost across geographic areas is called?
    a. Indemnity
    b. Service benefit plan
    c. UCR Fee
    d. Resource-based relative value scale

250. A process required by some insurance carriers where the provider obtains permission to perform certain procedures or services or refer a patient to a specialist is called?
    a. Pre-certification
    b. Pre-determination

c. Pre-authorization
d. Pre-verification

Test 1 Ans	
1	D
2	B
3	B
4	C
5	B
6	C
7	A
8	C
9	D
10	A
11	B
12	A
13	B
14	D
15	D
16	B
17	D
18	C
19	A
20	A
21	D
22	C
23	D
24	B
25	B
26	C
27	B
28	A
29	B

30	D
31	B
32	B
33	C
34	C
35	A
36	B
37	D
38	A
39	A
40	B
41	C
42	C
43	D
44	A
45	B
46	A
47	C
48	C
49	A
50	D
51	B
52	A
53	A
54	C
55	C
56	C
57	C
58	B
59	D
60	C
61	C

62	D
63	B
64	B
65	D
66	B
67	D
68	D
69	A
70	B
71	D
72	C
73	D
74	A
75	D
76	C
77	B
78	D
79	A
80	A
81	C
82	C
83	A
84	C
85	D
86	C
87	C
88	B
89	B
90	A
91	B
92	D
93	C

94	B
95	C
96	C
97	D
98	B
99	B
100	A
101	D
102	C
103	B
104	C
105	C
106	D
107	B
108	A
109	A
110	B
111	C
112	A
113	A
114	D
115	B
116	B
117	C
118	C
119	B
120	**D**
121	C
122	A
123	C
124	D
125	A

126	D
127	B
128	D
129	A
130	B
131	B
132	A
133	C
134	A
135	B
136	A
137	C
138	D
139	D
140	D
141	C
142	A
143	D
144	C
145	B
146	A
147	D
148	A
149	D
150	D
151	A
152	B
153	B
154	A
155	C
156	C
157	B

158	C
159	A
160	A
161	D
162	D
163	C
164	D
165	A
166	A
167	D
168	A
169	C
170	A
171	A
172	A
173	B
174	D
175	C
176	B
177	B
178	D
179	D
180	C
181	D
182	B
183	B
184	A
185	B
186	C
187	D
188	A
189	C

190	D
191	C
192	A
193	C
194	A
195	B
196	B
197	A
198	B
199	D
200	D
201	D
202	B
203	C
204	B
205	A
206	B
207	A
208	A
209	C
210	C
211	B
212	D
213	A
214	C
215	A
216	B
217	C
218	D
219	D
220	C
221	D

222	C
223	C
224	B
225	A
226	B
227	A
228	C
229	D
230	A
231	B
232	D
233	C
234	B
235	D
236	B
237	C
238	C
239	C
240	B
241	B
242	C
243	D
244	D
245	B
246	A
247	D
248	C
249	D
250	C

Test 2

1. Which of this is not a useful skill for physically active learning?
    a. Walking and talking aloud while studying
    b. Using pictures to represent materials being studied
    c. Getting anxious while studying
    d. Over-learning a topic

2. Which of this is not a method of remembering materials taught in class?
    a. Quickly reviewing materials after class
    b. Creating songs for materials learnt
    c. Teaching it to someone else
    d. Studying another material when you don't understand the one being taught

3. _____ is not a Mind map that helps consolidate complex details and organize them in a format easy to remember?
    a. Spider Map
    b. Octopus Map
    c. Chain of event Map
    d. Fish-bone Map

4. _____ is a key to critical thinking?
   a. Reflection
   b. Learning
   c. Information
   d. Knowledge

5. The way an individual perceives and processes information to learn new material is called?
   a. Perceiving
   b. Processing
   c. Learning style
   d. Critical thinking

6. The constant practice of considering all aspects of a situation when deciding what to believe or what to do is called?
   a. Professional Behavior
   b. Reflection
   c. Critical thinking
   d. Learning Style

7. The process of considering new information and internalizing it to create new ways of examining information is called?
   a. Processing
   b. Examining
   c. Reflection

d. Perceiving

8. How an individual internalizes new information and makes it his or her own is called?
    a. Processing
    b. Examining
    c. Reflection
    d. Perceiving

9. The actions that identify the medical assistant as a member of a healthcare profession including being dependable, performing respectful patient care, demonstrating positive attitude and using teamwork is called?
    a. Healthcare behaviors
    b. Professional behaviors
    c. Medical Assistant actions
    d. Successful medical assistant student

10. For you to learn new materials you must _____ and _____ information?
    a. Perceive and Process
    b. Investigate and Learn
    c. Access and Examine
    d. Internalize and Perceive

11. Learners perceive information in 2 ways?

a. Active and passive
b. Appropriate and inappropriate
c. Learnt and Unlearnt
d. Concrete and Abstract

12. Learners with a concrete reflective style like to?
    a. Consider a situation from many different point of view
    b. Learn lots of facts and arrange new materials in a logical and clear manner
    c. Know how techniques and ideas work
    d. Relate new materials to other areas in their life

13. Learners with an Abstract reflective style like to?
    a. Consider a situation from many different point of view
    b. Learn lots of facts and arrange new materials in a logical and clear manner
    c. Know how techniques and ideas work
    d. Relate new materials to other areas in their life

14. Learners with a concrete active style like to?
    a. Consider a situation from many different point of view

b. Learn lots of facts and arrange new materials in a logical and clear manner

c. Know how techniques and ideas work

d. Relate new materials to other areas in their life

15. Which of this is not a time management skill?

a. Setting aside time to do things you enjoy

b. Avoid working on long term goals

c. Identify your main concern

d. Determining your purpose

16. An enzymatically controlled transformation of an organic compound is called?

a. Contamination

b. Fermentation

c. Organic

d. All of the above

17. A type of alternative medicine that attempts to stimulate the body to recover itself is called?

a. Naturopathy

b. Homeopathy

c. Osteopathic

d. Hospice

18. Slight misalignment of the vertebrae or partial dislocation is?
    a. Sprain
    b. Strain
    c. Subluxation
    d. Sublimation

19. The use of telecommunications devices to enhance and improve the results of radiologic procedures is?
    a. Telemedicine
    b. Teleradiology
    c. Televice
    d. All of the above

20. A condition in which majority of the people in a country or a geographical area are affected is called?
    a. Endemic
    b. Pandemic
    c. Osteopathic
    d. Mysticism

21. The experience of seeming to have direct communication with God or ultimate reality is?
    a. Mystery
    b. Spirituality
    c. Holistic

d. Mysticism

22. Which of this eradication is the greatest accomplishment of World Health Organization (WHO)?
    a. Polio
    b. Leprosy
    c. Chickenpox
    d. Smallpox

23. Which of these agencies created the ICD-9?
    a. United Nations
    b. World Health Organization
    c. U.S. Department of Health and Human Services
    d. National Institute of Health

24. _____ is the principal U.S agency for providing essential human services and protecting the health of all Americans?
    a. U.S Medical Institute
    b. World Health Organization
    c. U.S. Department of Health and Human Services (HHS)
    d. National Institute of Health

25. Which of the following is not pathogen studied at biosafety IV?
    a. Influenza virus
    b. Ebola Virus
    c. Lassa Virus
    d. Hantavirus

26. _____ is the principal U.S. federal agency concerned with the health and safety of people throughout the world as his part of HHS?
    a. United Nations
    b. World Health Organization
    c. Centers for Disease Control and Prevention
    d. National Institute of Health

27. Which of this is not a type of health care facility?
    a. Hospital
    b. Ambulatory care
    c. All of the above
    d. None of the above

28. Which of this is not a type of business structure that exists in the medical practice?
    a. Sole Proprietorship
    b. Limited Proprietorship

c. Partnership

d. Corporation

29. _____ is defined as an artificial entity having a legal and business status that is independent of its shareholders or employees?

 a. Sole Proprietorship

 b. Limited Proprietorship

 c. Partnership

 d. Corporation

30. Which of the following is the owner potentially liable for all of the acts of his or her professional employees and staff members?

 a. Sole Proprietorship

 b. Limited Proprietorship

 c. Partnership

 d. Corporation

31. Which of this has the disadvantage where each physician is liable for the actions and conduct of the other?

 a. Sole Proprietorship

 b. Limited Proprietorship

 c. Partnership

 d. Corporation

32. When an individual holds exclusive rights and title to all aspect of the medical practice is called?
    a. Sole Proprietorship
    b. Limited Proprietorship
    c. Partnership
    d. Corporation

33. This specialist uses radioactive substances for the diagnosis and treatment of diseases?
    a. Neurological Surgeon
    b. Nuclear Medicine Specialist
    c. Anesthesiologist
    d. Urologist

34. The medical specialist concerned with the treatment of disease and disorders of the urinary tract is?
    a. Neurological Surgeon
    b. Nuclear Medicine Specialist
    c. Anesthesiologist
    d. Urologist

35. Those concerned with the preventing the occurrence of both mental and physical illness and disability is?
    a. Physiatrist

b. Pathologist

c. Otolaryngologist

d. Preventive Medicine Specialist

36. The physicians that treats diseases and conditions that affects the ears, eyes and throat and structures relating to the head and neck is called?
    a. Thoracic Surgeon
    b. Pathologist
    c. Otolaryngologist
    d. Preventive Medicine Specialist

37. Those concerned with the operative treatment of the chest and chest wall, lungs and respiratory passages are called?
    a. Thoracic Surgeon
    b. Pathologist
    c. Otolaryngologist
    d. Preventive Medicine Specialist

38. The _____ are trained to locate subluxation and remove them using touch and x-ray films thereby restoring the normal flow of nerve energy so that the entire body can function in optimal fashion?
    a. Subluxationist
    b. Nerve Specialist

c. Chiropractor

d. Osteopathic

39. The doctor educated in caring for the feet including surgical treatment is called?
    a. Pathologist
    b. Footologist
    c. Dermatologist
    d. Podiatrist

40. Which of this is not a Licensed Medical Professional?
    a. Physician Assistants
    b. Nurse Practitioner
    c. Registered Nurse
    d. None of the above

41. Which of this is a type of ambulatory care?
    a. Physicians' offices
    b. Group Practices
    c. Multispecialty group
    d. All of the above

42. A type of medicine based on the theory that disturbances in the musculoskeletal system affect other bodily parts causing many disorders that can be corrected by various

manipulative techniques in conjunction with conventional medicine surgical and other therapeutic procedures is called?

   a. Chiropractor

   b. Osteopathic

   c. Neurological surgeon

   d. General Surgeon

43. The two major categories of duties of the medical assistance includes?

   a. Receiving and making calls

   b. Filing and retrieving records

   c. Administrative and clinical

   d. None of the above

44. The medical administrative assistant is employed to perform a wide array of duties in various health professions. Which of these is not a major duty?

   a. Management of correspondence

   b. Prepare patient's Bill of Right

   c. Scheduling

   d. Telephone Coverage

45. Which of these areas of medical assistance involves patient contact and assisting physicians in the back office?

a. Administrative
b. Health
c. Assistantship
d. Clinical

46. Which of this is not an area where the Medical assistance can work?
    a. Physician's office
    b. Insurance Companies
    c. Hospitals
    d. None of the above

47. Which of this is an unacceptable behavior for the medical assistance on the externship site?
    a. Handling petty cash in the office
    b. Asking the physician to treat you or family members
    c. Respecting patient's confidentiality
    d. None of the above

48. Which of the following is true about the CMA and RMA?
    a. CMA and RMA certification are awarded by the same agency
    b. CMA and RMA are both nationally recognized certification
    c. All of the above

d. None of the above

49. Disobedience to authority is known as?
    a. Insubordination
    b. Non-professionalism
    c. Subordination
    d. Improper

50. _____ is defined as exhibiting a courteous, conscientious and generally businesslike manner in the workplace?
    a. Courteousness
    b. Professionalism
    c. Work ethics
    d. Principles

51. Which of this trait alone can influence promotion, termination and the entire atmosphere of the office?
    a. Attitude
    b. Courtesy
    c. Flexibility
    d. Confidentiality

52. What does Work smart mean?
    a. Teamwork
    b. Time management
    c. Using initiative

d. All of the above

53. Which of this is not a characteristic of professionalism?
    a. Dependability
    b. Flexibility
    c. Credibility
    d. None of the above

54. _____ is an offensive or use of force on a person without his or her consent?
    a. Battery
    b. Offense
    c. Illegal
    d. Defense

55. _____ is the study of the nature, degree and effect if the spatial separation individuals naturally maintain?
    a. Perception
    b. Space
    c. Proxemics
    d. Nonverbal Communication

56. _____ is the process of converting a message into an intelligible form; recognizes and interprets?
    a. Encoding
    b. Decoding
    c. Recording
    d. Interpreting

57. _____ is the process of converting from one system of communication to another; converts a message to a code?
    a. Encoding
    b. Decoding
    c. Recording
    d. Interpreting

58. _____ is the process, function or power of perceiving sounds?
    a. Listening
    b. Speaking
    c. Hearing
    d. Perceiving

59. _____ is defined as paying attention to sound or hearing something with thoughtful attention?
    a. Listening

b. Speaking

c. Hearing

d. Perceiving

60. _____ is the skill whereby paraphrasing and clarifying what the speaker has said take place?

   a. Passive Listening

   b. Active Listening

   c. Paraphrasing

   d. Analyzing

61. _____ is listening to what the sender is communicating, analyzing the words and restating them to confirm that the receiver has understood the message as the sender intended?

   a. Passive Listening

   b. Hearing

   c. Paraphrasing

   d. Analyzing

62. Which form of question is best to ask patients?

   a. Open

   b. Closed

   c. All of the above

   d. None of the above

63. _____ is the reversion to an earlier mental or behavioral level?

    a. Repression

    b. Regression

    c. Rationalization

    d. Suppression

64. The process whereby unwanted desires or impulses are excluded from the consciousness and left to operate in the unconscious is called?

    a. Repression

    b. Regression

    c. Rationalization

    d. Suppression

65. _____ is a lack of feeling, emotion, interest or concern. An indifference to what is happening or a pretense of not caring about a situation?

    a. Repression

    b. Denial

    c. Apathy

    d. Suppression

66. _____ is a psychologic defense mechanism in which confrontation with a personal problem or with reality is avoided by

denying the existence of the problem or reality?

    a. Repression

    b. Denial

    c. Apathy

    d. Suppression

67. _____ is defined as the struggle resulting from incompatible or opposing needs, drives, wishes or external or internal demands?

    a. Aggression

    b. Violence

    c. Conflict

    d. Opposition

68. According to Bach in the concept of "crazymaker" which of this is not a characteristic type of passive-aggressive person?

    a. The Attacker

    b. The Trapper

    c. The Avoider

    d. The Mind Reader

69. Instead of allowing their partners to express feelings of honesty the _____ go into character analysis, explaining what the other

person really mean or what is wrong with the other person?

    a. The Attacker

    b. The Trapper

    c. The Avoider

    d. The Mind Reader

70. Because they are afraid to face conflicts squarely, the _____ kid around when their partners want to be serious, thus blocking the expression of important feelings?

    a. The Trivial Tyrannizer

    b. The Distractor

    c. The Joker

    d. The Crisis Tickler

71. The _____ brings what is bothering them almost to the surface but never quite expressing their true feelings?

    a. The Trivial Tyrannizer

    b. The Distractor

    c. The Joker

    d. The Crisis Tickler

72. Instead of honestly sharing their resentments, the _____ do things they know will bother their partners?

a. The Trivial Tyrannizer

b. The Distractor

c. The Joker

d. The Crisis Tickler

73. The _____ will not allow their relationship to change from the way they once were?

    a. The Kitchen sink fighter

    b. The Contract Tyrannizer

    c. The Withholder

    d. The Beltliner

74. The _____ brings up things that are totally off the subject when in an argument?

    a. The Kitchen sink fighter

    b. The Contract Tyrannizer

    c. The Withholder

    d. The Beltliner

75. Instead of expressing their anger honestly and directly, the _____ punish their partners by holding something back?

    a. The Kitchen sink fighter

    b. The Contract Tyrannizer

    c. The Withholder

    d. The Beltliner

76. _____ is defined as the application of a standardized mental picture that is held in common by members of a group and that represents an oversimplified opinion, prejudiced attitude or uncritical judgment?
    a. Stereotyping
    b. Discrimination
    c. Perception
    d. Prejudice

77. The discernment of what is being communicated according to the message receiver's point of reference is known as?
    a. Stereotyping
    b. Discrimination
    c. Perception
    d. Prejudice

78. Maslow believes that our human needs can be categorized into _____ levels and that the needs on each level must be satisfied before we can move to the next level?
    a. 3
    b. 4
    c. 5
    d. 7

79. On what level does safety and security fall in Maslow's hierarchy of needs?
    a. 1st
    b. 2nd
    c. 3rd
    d. 4th

80. On what level does self-esteem and self-recognition fall in Maslow's hierarchy of needs?
    a. 1st
    b. 2nd
    c. 3rd
    d. 4th

81. Which of this sleep phases are the eyes fairly still and the body relaxes and slows down?
    a. Eye movement
    b. Rapid Eye Movement
    c. Non-Rapid Eye Movement
    d. Deep Sleep

82. Which of this is not a barrier to effective communication?
    a. Physical impairment
    b. Language Differences
    c. Prejudice
    d. None of the above

83. Which level does sleep fall under Maslow's hierarchy of needs?
    a. 1st
    b. 2nd
    c. 3rd
    d. 4th

84. _____ is defined as the thoughts, judgments and actions on issues that have implications of moral right and wrong?
    a. Conduct
    b. Ethics
    c. Principles
    d. Etiquette

85. Refraining from the act of harming or committing evil is called?
    a. Maleficence
    b. Nonmaleficence
    c. Beneficence
    d. Benevolent

86. The act of doing or producing good, especially of performing acts of charity or kindness is?
    a. Maleficence
    b. Nonmaleficence

    c. Beneficence

    d. Favor

87. Faithfulness to something to which one is bounded by pledge or duty is called?

    a. Veracity

    b. Disposition

    c. Fidelity

    d. Benevolence

88. The act or practice of killing or permitting the death of hopelessly sick or injured individuals in a relatively painless way for reason of mercy is?

    a. Euthanasia

    b. Postmortem

    c. Ramifications

    d. Abortion

89. Which of this is not a type of ethical problem presented by Purtilo?

    a. Ethical Distress

    b. Ethical Dilemmas

    c. Dilemmas of Justice

    d. Distress of Justice

90. _____ is a situation in which an individual is faced with two or more choices

that are acceptable and correct but doing one thing precludes doing another?

   a. Ethical Distress

   b. Ethical Dilemmas

   c. Dilemmas of Justice

   d. Distress of Justice

91. The type of problem faced when a certain course of action is indicated, but some type of hindrance or barrier prevents that action?

   a. Ethical Distress

   b. Ethical Dilemmas

   c. Dilemmas of Justice

   d. Distress of Justice

92. An intentional, unlawful attempt of bodily injury to another by force is called?

   a. Assault

   b. Battery

   c. Act

   d. Felony

93. Presumed such as when a patient offers an arm for a phlebotomy procedure is called?

   a. Implied consent

   b. Unimplied consent

   c. Informed consent

   d. Uninformed consent

94. A consent usually written which states understanding of what treatment is to be undertaken and of the risk involved, why it should be done and alternative treatment available is called?
    a. Implied consent
    b. Unimplied consent
    c. Informed consent
    d. Uninformed consent

95. A written defamatory statement or representation that conveys an unjust and unfavorable impression is called?
    a. Assault
    b. Slander
    c. Libel
    d. Defamation

96. An oral defamatory; a harmful false statement made about another person is?
    a. Assault
    b. Slander
    c. Libel
    d. Defamation

97. A binding custom or practice of a community; a rule of conduct or action prescribed or formally recognized as binding or enforceable by a controlling authority is called?

    a. Rules
    b. Regulations
    c. Law
    d. Conduct

98. A neutral person chosen to settle differences between two parties in a controversy is?

    a. Appellate
    b. Arbitrator
    c. Jury
    d. 3rd Party

99. A person required to make answer in a legal action or suit, in criminal cases, the person accused of a crime is?

    a. Plaintiff
    b. Defendant
    c. Suspect
    d. Respondent

100.   The person required to make answer in a civil legal action or suit is?

    a. Plaintiff
    b. Defendant

c. Suspect

d. Respondent

101.   Which of this is not a basic category of jurisprudence?

   a. Criminal law

   b. Civil law

   c. Tort law

   d. None of the above

102.   _____ law governs violations of the law that are punishable as offenses against the state or the government?

   a. Criminal law

   b. Civil law

   c. Tort law

   d. Administrative law

103.   Which of this is not a basic category of Criminal law?

   a. Misdemeanors

   b. Felonies

   c. Treasons

   d. Infractions

104.   The offense of attempting to overthrow the government is?

a. Misdemeanors

b. Felonies

c. Treasons

d. Infractions

105.   A minor crime punishable by fine or imprisonment in a city or county jail rather than in a penitentiary is?

a. Misdemeanors

b. Felonies

c. Treasons

d. Infractions

106.   _____ law provides a remedy for a person or group that has suffered harm from the wrongful act of others?

a. Contract Law

b. Administrative Law

c. Tort Law

d. Justice Law

107.   A list of questions from each party to the other in a law suit is?

a. Interrogatories

b. Questioning

c. Inquiring

d. Probing

108.   A document issued by a court requiring a person to be in court at a specific time and place to testify as a witness in a lawsuit either in a court proceeding or in a deposition is?
   a. Subpoenas
   b. Command
   c. Order
   d. Summon

109.   A bench trial is?
   a. When the case is open and the defendant is absent
   b. When a case is decided by the judge in the absence of a jury
   c. When a case is on probation
   d. None of the above

110.   The performance of an act that is wholly wrongful and unlawful is?
   a. Nonfeasance
   b. Disfeasance
   c. Malfeasance
   d. Misfeasance

111.   The failure to perform an act that should have been performed is?
   a. Nonfeasance

b. Disfeasance

c. Malfeasance

d. Misfeasance

112.   The improper performance of a lawful act is?

a. Nonfeasance

b. Disfeasance

c. Malfeasance

d. Misfeasance

113.   Which of this is not part of the "4 D's of negligence"?

a. Damage

b. Danger

c. Direct cause

d. Duty

114.   Which of the "4 D's of negligence" must there be proof that the harm done to the patient was directly caused by the physicians action or failure to act?

a. Damage

b. Danger

c. Direct cause

d. Duty

115. Which of the "4 D's of negligence" must the patient proof that a loss or harm has resulted from the actions of the physician?
   a. Damage
   b. Danger
   c. Direct cause
   d. Duty

116. Which of this is not a type of damage seen in tort cases?
   a. Minimal
   b. Special
   c. General
   d. Punitive

117. _____ damages are designed to punish party who committed the wrong in such a way as to deter the repetition of the act?
   a. Compensatory
   b. Special
   c. Nominal
   d. Punitive

118. _____ damages are those injuries or losses that are not a necessary consequence of the physician's negligent act or omission?
   a. Compensatory
   b. Special

c. General

d. Punitive

119.   Damages that includes compensation for pain and suffering, for loss of a bodily member or faculty, for disfigurement or for other similar direct losses or injuries is?
   a. Compensatory
   b. Special
   c. General
   d. Punitive

120.   Exemplary damages can also be called?
   a. Compensatory
   b. Special
   c. General
   d. Punitive

121.   A period of time after which a lawsuit cannot be filed is?
   a. Statute of Fraud
   b. Statute of Unfiling
   c. Statute of Limitation
   d. Statute of Restrain

122.   Which of this is not a patient's bill of right?

a. Respect and Nondiscrimination
b. Complaints and Appeals
c. Choice of providers and plans
d. None of the above

123. Which of this is not a benefit of the HIPAA compliance?
    a. Lowers administrative cost
    b. Increases accuracy of data
    c. Reduces revenue cycle time
    d. None of the above

124. _____ is responsible for the identification of the various hazards present in the workplace and for the creation of rules and regulations to minimize exposure to such hazards?
    a. Employees
    b. Employers
    c. HIPAA
    d. OSHA

125. _____ are mandated to institute measures that will assure safe working conditions and health workers have the obligation to know and follow those measures?
    a. Employees

b. Employers

c. HIPAA

d. OSHA

126. A needle and sharp stick injury log must at a minimum include the following except?
   a. Description of the incident
   b. Type and brand of device used
   c. Time of the incident
   d. Location of the incident

127. The hepatitis B Vaccination must be taken by all employees with the first 10days of work for risk of occupational exposure, who is responsible for the cost?
   a. Employees
   b. Employers
   c. CLIA
   d. OSHA

128. For a valid contract to exist there has to be?
   a. A offer
   b. An acceptance
   c. All of the above
   d. None of the above

129.   The Americans with Disability Act requires that public medical facilities must allow persons with disabilities to do the following except?
   a. Use drinking fountains, phones and hallways
   b. Do everything that the general public is able to do in the public place
   c. Reach door handles for opening and closing
   d. None of the above

130.   Which of this is not a ground for the revocation or suspension of the license to practice medicine?
   a. Personal or professional incapacity
   b. Unprofessional conduct
   c. Conviction of a crime
   d. Arrest

131.   Which type of civil law deals with medical professional liability?
   a. Contract Law
   b. Administrative Law
   c. Tort Law
   d. Justice Law

132. Which of this is not an essential element needed for a valid contract?
   a. Manifestation of assent
   b. Contract must involve legal subject matter
   c. Parties to the contract do not need legal capacity to enter into the contract
   d. None of the above

133. Any type of storage of files to prevent their loss in the event of hard disk failure in the future is called?
   a. Backup
   b. Hard disk
   c. Hard drive
   d. Software

134. The smallest units of information inside the computer each represented by either the digit "0" or "1" is?
   a. Kilobyte
   b. Byte
   c. Bite
   d. Bits

135.   A unit of data that contains 8 binary digit is?

    a. Kilobyte

    b. Byte

    c. Bite

    d. Bits

136.   A device that is capable of "writing" data onto a blank compact disk or copying data from one compact disk to a blank compact is called?

    a. Data writer

    b. CD writer

    c. CD

    d. CD Burner

137.   A machine designed to accept, store, process and give out information is?

    a. Printer

    b. Computer

    c. Processor

    d. HP

138.   A symbol appearing on the monitor that shows where the next character to be typed will appear is?

    a. Space

    b. Cursor

c. Line

d. Margin

139. The nonphysical space appearing of the online world of computer networks in which communication takes place is?

    a. Online space
    b. Cyberspace
    c. Internet space
    d. Nonphysical space

140. A collection of data related files that serves as a foundation for retrieving information is?

    a. Computer
    b. Backup
    c. Database
    d. Microsoft word

141. DVD means?

    a. Digital video drive
    b. Driver video disk
    c. Digital video disk
    d. Disk video drive

142.   A removable device shaped like a hard plastic square with a magnetic surface that is capable of storing computer program is?
   a. Disk drives
   b. Hard drive
   c. Disk
   d. DVD

143.   Device that loads a program or data stored on a disk into the computer is?
   a. Disk drives
   b. Hard drive
   c. Disk
   d. DVD

144.   _____ is also called a diskette?
   a. Disk drive
   b. Hard drive
   c. Disk
   d. DVD

145.   An optical disk that holds approximately 28 times more information that a compact disk is?
   a. CD
   b. Hard drive
   c. DVD

d. Flash Drive

146.   Fax is an abbreviation for?
   a. Faxing
   b. Facsimile
   c. Duplicating
   d. Telexing

147.   Animation technology used in the opening page of a website to draw attention, excite and impress the user is?
   a. Flash
   b. Animation
   c. Impress
   d. Web design

148.   A small portable device that connects into the USB port that can carry 2 to 8 or more gigabytes of information is?
   a. Floppy disk
   b. Zip drive
   c. Flash
   d. Flash drive

149.   A small portable disk drive that is primarily used for backing up information and archiving computer files is?

a. Floppy disk

b. Zip drive

c. Flash

d. Flash drive

150.   Approximately 1 billion byte is a?

a. Megabyte

b. Kilobyte

c. Milobyte

d. Gigabyte

151.   Approximately 1 million byte is a?

a. Megabyte

b. Kilobyte

c. Milobyte

d. Gigabyte

152.   A common connecting point for devices in a network containing multiple ports is?

a. Nub

b. Port

c. Hub

d. Modem

153.   HTTP means?

a. Hyper transfer text protocol

b. Hyper text transfer protocol

c. Hyper transfer text processor

d. Hyper text transfer processor

154. The physical component of the computer is the?
   a. Hardware
   b. Software
   c. Input
   d. Output

155. Pictures often on the desktop of a computer that represent programs or object is?
   a. Media
   b. Picture frame
   c. Programs
   d. Icons

156. MIDI is an acronym for?
   a. Midnight
   b. Midday
   c. Musical Interface Digital Instrument
   d. Musical Instrument Digital Interface

157. A device that allows information to be transmitted over telephone lines at speeds measured in bits per second is?
   a. Nub

b. Server

c. Hub

d. Modem

158. A computer or device on a network that manages shared network resources is?

a. Router

b. Server

c. Hub

d. Modem

159. A request for information from a database is?

a. Routing

b. Queries

c. Data request

d. Search engine

160. Information processed by the computer and transmitted to a monitor, printer or other device is?

a. Hardware

b. Software

c. Input

d. Output

161. Which of this is a basic function of the computer?
   a. Input
   b. Processing
   c. Storage
   d. All of the above

162. The desktop consist of the following except?
   a. Central Processing unit
   b. Mouse
   c. Monitor
   d. None of the above

163. Which of the following devices has embedded computer?
   a. Ultrasound unit
   b. Laptop
   c. Notebook
   d. PDA

164. _____ is the center unit of the computer
   a. Keyboard
   b. CPU
   c. Monitor
   d. Mouse

165.   The device used to display computer generated information is the?

a. Keyboard
b. CPU
c. Monitor
d. Mouse

166.   The primary text input of the computer is the?

a. Keyboard
b. CPU
c. Monitor
d. Mouse

167.   _____ is the main circuit board for the computer?

a. Disk drives
b. Motherboard
c. CD-ROM
d. Memory Card

168.   Which of this is not a peripheral device?

a. Scanners
b. Digital cameras
c. Zip drives
d. Keyboard

169.   A computer should be thought of as an additional worker in the office?
   a. True
   b. False
   c. At times
   d. None of the above

170.   Which of the following is not a type of printer?
   a. Dot Matrix
   b. Inkjet
   c. Laser
   d. None of the above

171.   Telephone calls can be an interruption of the work day for the medical assistant?
   a. True
   b. False
   c. Some times
   d. None of the above

172.   When handling the telephone, the mouthpiece should be approximately _____ from the lips?
   a. 1 inch
   b. 0.5 inch

c. 5 inches

d. 10 inches

173.   After removing the phone from its
cradle speak?

   a. After the caller speaks first

   b. After 10 sec

   c. Immediately

   d. As the caller is speaking

174.   STAT is an abbreviation for?

   a. Start

   b. Status

   c. System Transmitting at Time

   d. Immediately

175.   A change in pitch or loudness of the
voice is?

   a. Jargon

   b. Monotone

   c. Diction

   d. Inflection

176.   When a patient is inaudible you could
use a speakerphone?

   a. True

b. False

c. At times

d. None of the above

177. Never answer a telephone call on the first ring?

a. True

b. False

c. At times

d. None of the above

178. You can multitask while answering phone calls?

a. True

b. False

c. At times

d. None of the above

179. It is okay to pick up a phone once it rings and say "please hold" immediately when you are busy?

a. True

b. False

c. At times

d. None of the above

180.   The use of salutation is compulsory in telephone identification?
   a. True
   b. False
   c. At times
   d. None of the above

181.   Which of the following is to be considered when scheduling patients for appointment?
   a. Physicians preference and habit
   b. Patient needs
   c. Available facility
   d. All of the above

182.   The process of evaluating the urgency of medical need and prioritizing treatment is?
   a. Interval
   b. Intermittent
   c. Triage
   d. Proficiency

183.   Coming and going at intervals; not continuous is?
   a. Interval
   b. Intermittent
   c. Triage

d. Proficiency

184. Competency as a result of training or practice is?
   a. Interval
   b. Intermittent
   c. Triage
   d. Proficiency

185. One disadvantage of computer scheduling is that more than one person cannot access the system at the same time.
   a. True
   b. False
   c. At times
   d. None of the above

186. _____ method of scheduling appointments can also be referred to as tidal wave scheduling?
   a. Wave scheduling
   b. Scheduled Appointment
   c. Double booking
   d. Open office hours

187. Which of this is not a basic feature to consider when choosing an appointment book?
   a. It should be color coded

b. Size should conform to the desk space

c. It should open flat for easy writing

d. It should be large enough to accommodate the practice

188. Something in which a thing originates, develops, takes shape, or is contained; a base on which to build is called?

a. Integral

b. Matrix

c. Expediency

d. None of the above[

189. The medical administrative should consider the following characteristics when selecting an appointment book except:

a. Its size in consideration of the amount of desk space available

b. Comfort for writing

c. Number of pages

d. Adequate space for all details necessary

190. When certain number of patients are scheduled to arrive at the same time and are seen in the order in which they arrive is called?

a. Modified wave scheduling

b. Modified scheduling

c. Double Booking

d. Wave scheduling

191. Scheduling two patients to see the physician at the same time is?

a. Modified wave scheduling

b. Modified scheduling

c. Double Booking

d. Wave scheduling

192. Small groups of patients are scheduled at intervals throughout the hour is called?

a. Modified wave scheduling

b. Modified scheduling

c. Double Booking

d. Wave scheduling

193. The Medical Administrative Assistant should do the following when scheduling a new patient except

a. The Medical Assistant can schedule appointment time for patient solely in his/her discretion without the patient's consent

b. Gather appropriate information regarding a patient referral

139

c. Determine the proper financial arrangements for the patient's appointment

d. Determine the patient's chief complaint

194. The Medical Administrative Assistant should do the following when scheduling an established patient except:

a. Gather the appropriate information in order to properly identify the patient

b. Do without verification of information since they are established patient

c. Provide patient with appointment card if necessary

d. Enter the appropriate time for the appointment

195. Which of this is not a way in which the medical assistant can help prepare a patient for an examination?

a. Escort patient to the examination room and other areas of the office

b. Make sure that the patients wallet and other items are secured

c. Stay with the patient all through the examination and after

d. Ask whether the patient has any questions

196.   The following are ways to make patient feel at ease and comfortable in the medical office except?
   a. Personal touch
   b. Attractive reception
   c. Using the patient's name often
   d. None of the above

197.   A person who comes to a country to take up permanent residence is called?
   a. Permanent Resider
   b. Green card holder
   c. Immigrant
   d. Migrant

198.   A two way communication system with a microphone and loudspeaker at each station for localized used is?
   a. Headset
   b. Handset
   c. Intercom
   d. Starcom

199.   Notes used in the patient chart to track the progress and condition of the patient is called?
   a. Progress notes
   b. Patient chart book
   c. Patient file
   d. Patient record

200.   The statistical characteristics of human populations used especially to identify markets is called?
   a. Statistical data
   b. Population census
   c. Demographic
   d. All of the above

201.   An accounting period of 12 months during which a company determines earnings and profit is called?
   a. Annual year
   b. Fiscal year
   c. Profit sharing year
   d. None of the above

202.   The practice of subcontracting work to an outside company is called?
   a. Delegation

b. Subcontracting

c. Designating

d. Outsourcing

203.   Differences amongst conflicting facts, claims or opinions is called?

a. Differentiation

b. Discrepancies

c. Variety

d. Diversity

204.   Marking a document or a specific place within a document for later retrieval; a feature supported by most browsers that allows user to save the address so that the document can be located when it is needed again is?

a. Bookmark

b. History

c. Backmark

d. Saving document

205.   An order item that has not been delivered when promised or demanded but will be supplied at a later date is?

a. Backorder

b. Backlog

c. None Delivery

d. Failed promise

206.   A plan for the coordination of resources and expenditures; the amount of money that is available or required for a particular purpose is?
   a. Planning
   b. Organizing
   c. Budget
   d. Revenue

207.   A list of items that are included in a shipment is called?
   a. Shipment slip
   b. Packing slip
   c. Item list
   d. Invoice

208.   To become liable or subject to; to bring down on oneself is called?
   a. Humility
   b. Liability
   c. Self-esteem
   d. Incur

Acting in anticipation of future problems, needs or changes is?

    e. Action

    f. Inaction

    g. Proactive

    h. All of the above

209. When moving through hallways, the medical assistance should walk on the?

    a. Left side

    b. Right side

    c. Middle

    d. Anywhere

210. The office policy manual should be read?

    a. When the medical assistant begin work at the physician's office

    b. As a daily source of information for all employees to reference whenever needed

    c. At least annually

    d. All of the above

211. The office policy manual should include the following except?

    a. Sexual harassment

b. Vacations

c. Continuing education

d. Pay scale

212.   Below are some expenses that are involved in the operation of a medical practice except?

a. Taxes

b. Utilities

c. Medical equipment

d. Legal expenses

213.   An itemized list of goods shipped that specifies price and the term of sale is?

a. Invoice

b. Bill

c. Statement

d. Receipt

214.   A statement of financial account that shows the balance due as well as transactions that affects the account is?

a. Invoice

b. Bill

c. Statement

d. Receipt

215. The following are ways in which physician's office employees can reduce waste while saving money except?

    a. Use solar powered calculators and batter rechargers

    b. Use refillable pens and pencils

    c. Use bulletin board

    d. None of the above

216. In the case of a robbery, the medical assistance should make every effort to remember the following basic identification markers except?

    a. Hand

    b. Weight

    c. Race

    d. Clothing

217. For office security the alarm code should be known by?

    a. All staff members

    b. Only the office manager

    c. Only Physician

    d. The office manager and those who open and close the facility and physician

218. The use of fire extinguisher can be memorized using the mnemonics device PASS; the "P" means?
    a. Please
    b. Pull the pin
    c. Point of pulling
    d. Place to pull

219. The use of fire extinguisher can be memorized using the mnemonics device PASS; the "A" means?
    a. Act
    b. Action
    c. Aim the hose
    d. Arm the hose

220. The use of fire extinguisher can be memorized using the mnemonics device PASS; the first "S" means?
    a. Seize the nozzle
    b. Squeeze
    c. Sweep the nozzle
    d. Strip

221. The use of fire extinguisher can be memorized using the mnemonics device PASS; the second "S" means?

a. Seize the nozzle

b. Squeeze

c. Sweep the nozzle

d. Strip

222. _____ is the applied science concerned with designing and arranging things people use so that the people and the things interact efficiently and safely?

a. Ergonomics

b. Acoustics

c. White Noise

d. Audibility

223. _____ is defined as the science that deals with the production, control, transmission, reception, and effects of sound?

a. Ergonomics

b. Acoustics

c. White Noise

d. Audibility

224. The following actions are needed to be taken before the office opens in the morning except?

a. Office should be clean

b. Make two copies of the appointment book
c. Phones should be turned to answering machine
d. Exam room supplies should be checked and replaced when necessary

225. A durable, formal paper used for document is?
   a. Typing sheet
   b. A4 paper
   c. Bond
   d. Formal paper

226. Method of payment used when an article or item is delivered and payment is expected before released is?
   a. Collect on delivery
   b. Payment on delivery
   c. Delivered on payment
   d. All of the above

227. The receiver of something or item is?
   a. Acceptor
   b. Collector
   c. Recipient
   d. Heir

228.	A marking in paper resulting from differences in thickness usually produced by the pressure of a projecting design in the mold or on a processing roll and visible when the paper is held up to the light is?
   a.	Bookmark
   b.	Watermark
   c.	Papermark
   d.	Design mark

229.	Furnishing with notes that are usually critical or explanatory is?
   a.	Annotating
   b.	Noting
   c.	Appendix
   d.	Glossary

230.	Which of the nouns are specific?
   a.	Common noun
   b.	Proper noun
   c.	Pronoun
   d.	Specific noun

231.	Connecting words that shows a relationship between nouns, pronouns or other words in a sentence are called?

a. Adverb

b. Adjective

c. Preposition

d. Conjunction

232.   Which of the following is not a part of speech?

a. Verb

b. Sentence

c. Noun

d. Preposition

233.   Which of the following is not a type of sentence?

a. Declarative

b. Imperative

c. Statement

d. Exclamatory

234.   Which of this type of sentence states a command or request?

a. Declarative

b. Imperative

c. Statement

d. Exclamatory

235. Which of the following is not a basic pattern for constructing sentence?
   a. Subject predicate
   b. Subject object
   c. Subject complement
   d. None of the above

236. _____ is an incomplete thought or a portion of a sentence that is punctuated as though it were a complete sentence?
   a. Run on sentence
   b. Sentence fragment
   c. Comma splice
   d. Subject predicate

237. The part of a sentence that contains the verb and tells what the subject is doing or experiencing or what is being done to the subject is?
   a. Run on sentence
   b. Sentence fragment
   c. Comma splice
   d. Subject predicate

238. A sentence that contains independent clauses without a semicolon or comma between them is called?

a. Run on sentence

b. Sentence fragment

c. Comma splice

d. Subject predicate

239. _____ type of sentence is also called run-together?

a. Run on sentence

b. Sentence fragment

c. Comma splice

d. Subject predicate

240. When writing letter in a block letter style where should you have your signature located?

a. Top Right

b. Lower Right

c. Lower middle

d. Lower Left

241. When writing letter in a modified block letter style where should you have your signature located?

a. Top Right

b. Lower Right

c. Lower middle

d. Lower Left

242. Which of the following numbers will be filled Second?
   a. 4321234
   b. 4123453
   c. 3487631
   d. 4123443

243. Which of this names will be filled Third?
   a. Adam-Smith
   b. Adams
   c. Adamu
   d. Anna

244. First-class mail that weighs more than 13 ounces is called?
   a. Priority Mail
   b. Express Mail
   c. Certified Mail
   d. Bulk Mailing

245. This type of mail is available every day of the year, including holidays, for items up to 70 lbs in weight and 108 inches in height
   a. Priority Mail
   b. Express Mail
   c. Certified Mail

d. Bulk Mailing

246. This type of mailing gives the sender the option to receive proof of delivery?
    a. Media Mail
    b. Express Mail
    c. Certified Mail
    d. First class Mail

247. This type of mail includes letters, postal cards, postcards, and business reply mail?
    a. Media Mail
    b. Express Mail
    c. First class Mail
    d. Certified Mail

248. _____ is used for books, films, manuscripts, printed music, printed test materials, videotapes and computer recorded media
    a. Media Mail
    b. Express Mail
    c. First class Mail
    d. Certified Mail

249. Which of the following is not a basic size of envelop?

a. No. 10
b. No. 5
c. No. 6 ¾
d. Window

MA Test 2

1	C
2	D
3	B
4	A
5	C
6	C
7	C
8	A
9	B
10	A
11	D
12	A
13	B
14	D
15	B
16	A
17	B
18	C
19	B
20	B
21	D
22	D
23	B
24	C
25	A
26	C
27	D
28	B
29	D
30	A

31	C
32	A
33	B
34	D
35	D
36	C
37	A
38	C
39	D
40	D
41	D
42	B
43	C
44	B
45	D
46	D
47	B
48	B
49	A
50	B
51	A
52	B
53	D
54	A
55	C
56	B
57	A
58	C
59	A
60	B
61	C
62	A
63	B

64	A
65	C
66	B
67	C
68	A
69	D
70	C
71	D
72	A
73	B
74	A
75	C
76	A
77	C
78	C
79	B
80	D
81	C
82	D
83	A
84	B
85	B
86	C
87	C
88	A
89	D
90	B
91	A
92	A
93	A
94	C
95	C
96	B

97	C
98	B
99	B
100	D
101	C
102	A
103	D
104	C
105	A
106	C
107	A
108	A
109	B
110	C
111	A
112	D
113	B
114	C
115	A
116	A
117	D
118	B
119	C
120	D
121	C
122	D
123	D
124	D
125	B
126	C
127	B
128	C
129	D

130	D
131	C
132	C
133	A
134	D
135	B
136	D
137	B
138	B
139	B
140	C
141	C
142	C
143	A
144	C
145	C
146	B
147	A
148	D
149	B
150	D
151	A
152	C
153	B
154	A
155	D
156	D
157	D
158	B
159	B
160	D
161	D
162	D

163	A
164	B
165	C
166	A
167	B
168	D
169	A
170	D
171	B
172	A
173	C
174	D
175	D
176	B
177	B
178	B
179	B
180	B
181	D
182	C
183	B
184	D
185	B
186	D
187	A
188	B
189	C
190	D
191	C
192	A
193	A
194	B
195	C

196	D
197	C
198	C
199	A
200	C
201	B
202	D
203	B
204	A
205	A
206	C
207	B
208	D
209	C
210	B
211	D
212	D
213	D
214	A
215	C
216	C
217	A
218	D
219	B
220	C
221	B
222	C
223	A
224	B
225	C
226	C
227	A
228	C

229	B
230	A
231	B
232	C
233	B
234	C
235	B
236	D
237	B
238	D
239	A
240	A
241	D
242	C
243	D
244	C
245	A
246	B
247	C
248	C
249	A
250	B

Test 3

1. Any sustained, harmful alteration of the normal structure, function or metabolism of an organism or cell is called?
   a. Abnormal
   b. Structural deficiency
   c. Disease
   d. Virus

2. Which of the following is not part of the 5 groups of potentially pathogenic agent or microorganism?
   a. Rickettsia
   b. Protozoa
   c. Bacteria
   d. Antigens

3. All but one is not a component of the chain of infection?
   a. Susceptible host
   b. Portal of Settlement
   c. Agent
   d. Mode of transmission

4. _____ are infectious microorganisms that can be classified into groups namely: viruses, bacteria, fungi, and parasites?
   a. Portal of exit

b. Patients

c. Agents

d. Portal of entry

5. Which of these is a mode of transmission?
   a. Contact : direct and indirect
   b. Droplet
   c. Airborne
   d. All of the above

6. What is the most important means of preventing the spread of infection?
   a. Medical Asepsis
   b. Barrier Protection
   c. Hand washing
   d. Isolation Precautions

7. The method by which an infectious agent leaves its reservoir is called?
   a. Portal of exit
   b. Patients
   c. Leaving Agents
   d. Portal of entry

8. When an infectious agent is allowed to access susceptible host is?
   a. Contact : direct and indirect
   b. Portal of exit
   c. Portal of entry
   d. Mode of transmission

9. When an infectious agent enters a person who is not resistant or immune is called?
    a. Contact : direct and indirect
    b. Susceptible host
    c. Portal of entry
    d. Mode of transmission

10. _____ is the destruction of pathogenic microorganisms after they leave the body?
    a. Medical Asepsis
    b. Barrier Protection
    c. Hand washing
    d. Isolation Precautions

11. Which of the following is not a portal of exit?
    a. Open wounds
    b. Head
    c. Eye
    d. Nose

12. Which of this is not an indirect transmission?
    a. Clapping
    b. Sneezing
    c. Speaking
    d. Coughing

13. Which of the following is not a type of infection?
    a. Acute infection
    b. Chronic infection
    c. Critical infection
    d. Slow infection

14. Which of this infection persist for a long period of time, sometimes for life?
    a. Acute infection
    b. Chronic infection
    c. Critical infection
    d. Slow infection

15. Which of this infections progress over very long period and are typically referred to as viral infection of the brain?
    a. Acute infection
    b. Latent infection
    c. Critical infection
    d. Slow infection

16. Personal Protective Equipment includes all EXCEPT?
    a. Masks
    b. Goggles
    c. Respirator
    d. Trash Bags

17. Which of the following is not a necessary use of gloves?
    a. Touching a patient's blood
    b. Welcoming a patient
    c. Performing Venipuncture
    d. Handling items and surfaces contaminated with blood and body fluid

18. Which of this is not a procedure to be followed if a worker is exposed through an accidental needlestick, human bite or broken skin?
    a. Apply pressure on the area
    b. Wash the exposed area
    c. File incident report on the exposed incident
    d. None of the above

19. _____ means freedom from infection or infectious material?
    a. Hepatitis B Vaccination
    b. Immunization
    c. Asepsis
    d. None of the above

20. Which of this is not a type of bacterial on the skin?
    a. Transient
    b. Follicle
    c. Resident
    d. None of the above

21._____ is the destruction of organisms before they enter the body?
   a. Surgical Asepsis
   b. Medical Asepsis
   c. Sanitization
   d. All of the above

22. The cleansing process that decreases the number of microorganism to a safe level as dictated in public health guidelines is?
   a. Surgical Asepsis
   b. Medical Asepsis
   c. Sanitization
   d. All of the above

23. The process of killing pathogenic organisms or of rendering them inactive is?
   a. Sanitizing
   b. Disinfection
   c. Sterilization
   d. None of the above

24. Foreign substance that causes the production of a specific antibody is called?
   a. Antibody
   b. Antigen
   c. Antiseptics
   d. Disinfectant

25. Agents that destroy pathogenic organism is called?
   a. Antiseptics
   b. Disinfectant
   c. Germicides
   d. Candidiasis

26. Infection caused by a yeast that typically affects the vaginal mucosa and skin is?
   a. Antiseptics
   b. Disinfectant
   c. Germicides
   d. Candidiasis

27. In the Medical Terminology what are some combining forms for HEAD?
   a. Cephal/o
   b. Cerebr/o
   c. Hepat/o
   d. Cyt/o

28. In the Medical Terminology what are the meaning of this combining forms Nephr/o
   a. Head
   b. Kidney
   c. Disease
   d. Flesh

29. In the Medical Terminology the suffix "-esis" means?
    a. Inflammation
    b. Protein
    c. Condition
    d. Disease

30. In the Medical Terminology the suffix "-dynia" means?
    a. Blood Condition
    b. Die
    c. Two
    d. Pain

31. In the Medical Terminology the suffix "-tomy" means?
    a. Cutting
    b. Clot
    c. Stomach
    d. Poison

32. In the Medical Terminology the suffix "-tripsy" means?
    a. Recording
    b. Excision
    c. Crushing
    d. Falling

33. _____ is a documentation form that introduces a logical sequence to recording the information obtained from a patient?
   a. SOMR
   b. POMR
   c. EMR
   d. Logical record keeping

34. The "E" in "SOAPE" means?
   a. Emergency
   b. Electronic
   c. Evaluation
   d. Ethical

35. The "P" in "POMR" means?
   a. Process
   b. Principles
   c. Plan
   d. Problem

36. The "O" in "POMR" means?
   a. Organize
   b. Oriented
   c. Option
   d. Opportunity

37. The "M" in "POMR" means?
   a. Means
   b. Method

c. Medical

d. Maintain

38. The "R" in "POMR" means?

    a. Record

    b. Resources

    c. Rights

    d. Relationship

39. The "S" in "SOMR" means?

    a. Sort

    b. Source

    c. Sign

    d. Solution

40. Which of these is not part of the holistic model in developing an effective teaching approach for patients?

    a. Physical

    b. Biological

    c. Spiritual

    d. Social

41. Patient education should begin with the first contact between the patient and the?

    a. Cleaners

    b. Janitors

    c. Healthcare team

    d. Other patients

42. Which of the following is a guideline for patient education that can affect the overall wellness of patient wellness?
    a. Provide knowledge and skill that promote recovery
    b. Encourage healthy behaviors
    c. Include family in education intervention
    d. All of the above

43. Which of these patient factors has an impact on learning?
    a. Age and developmental level
    b. Influence of multicultural and diversity factors
    c. Individual learning style
    d. All of the above

44. Which of these is a potential barrier to patient's learning?
    a. Patient motivation to learn
    b. Limited time for teaching
    c. Physical limitation
    d. All of the above

45. Which of this is not a teaching material and method that are effective for individual patient needs?
    a. Videos
    b. Approved internet sites

c. Journals of events

d. None of the above

46. _____ refers to all the processes involved in the intake and use of nutrients?

a. Nutrition

b. Nutrients

c. Anabolism

d. Metabolism

47. _____ are the organic and inorganic chemicals in food that supply the energy and raw materials for cellular activities?

a. Nutrition

b. Nutrients

c. Anabolism

d. Metabolism

48. The process in which nutrients are used at the cellular level for growth and energy production as well as excretion of waste?

a. Nutrition

b. Nutrients

c. Anabolism

d. Metabolism

49. Which of this is not a nutrient?

a. Fat

b. Vitamins

c. Minerals

d. None of the above

50. The building phase in which smaller molecules combine to form larger molecules is called?
    a. Nutrition
    b. Nutrients
    c. Anabolism
    d. Metabolism

51. The breaking-down phase in which larger molecules are broken down and converted into smaller units is called?
    a. Digestion
    b. Dietetics
    c. Catabolism
    d. Anabolism

52. The combination of mechanical and chemical processes occurring in the mouth, stomach and small intestine that results in reducing nutrients into absorbable forms is?
    a. Digestion
    b. Dietetics
    c. Catabolism
    d. Anabolism

53. The practical application of nutritional science to individual is called?
    a. Digestion
    b. Dietetics

c. Catabolism

d. Anabolism

54. The amount of energy needed to maintain essential body function is?
    a. Basal metabolism
    b. Catabolism
    c. Anabolism
    d. All of the above

55. _____ is commonly called roughages?
    a. Carbohydrates
    b. Dietary fibers
    c. Plants
    d. Fruits

56. The portion of the plant that cannot be digested or absorbed is called?
    a. Carbohydrates
    b. Dietary fibers
    c. Plants
    d. Fruits

57. If fatty acids have one unfilled hydrogen bond, the fat is called?
    a. Mono fatty acid
    b. Monosaturated
    c. Monounsaturated
    d. Polysaturated

58. A _____ molecule is created when three fatty acid attach to a molecule of glycerol?
   a. Protein
   b. Dietary fats
   c. Hydrogenated fat
   d. Triglyceride

59. Which of this is not a place where the body stores fat?
   a. Hips
   b. Abdomen
   c. Arms
   d. None of the above

60. The relationship of weight to height, and its mathematical correlation of the patient's measurement with health risk is?
   a. Body Mass Index
   b. Body Fat Measurement
   c. Body health risk
   d. None of the above

61. The BMI is calculated as?
   a. $\dfrac{\text{Height (kg)} \times 100}{\text{Weight (m)}}$
   b. Height X Weight
   c. $\dfrac{\text{Height (kg)}}{\text{Weight (m)}}$
   d. $\dfrac{\text{Height X Weight}}{100}$

62. Which of this is not a type of surgery procedure performed for severely obese person?
   a. Restrictive
   b. Malabsorptive
   c. Restrictive Malabsorptive
   d. None of the above

63. The surgical procedure for the obese that decreases the size of the stomach and slows the movement of food through it is?
   a. Restrictive
   b. Malabsorptive
   c. Restrictive Malabsorptive
   d. None of the above

64. _____ is defined as the physical exertion for the maintenance or improvement of health or for the correction of a physical handicap?
   a. Eating well balanced diet
   b. Good rest
   c. Exercise
   d. All of the above

65. Organic compound that forms the chief constituent of protein and are used by the body to build and repair tissue is called?
   a. Organic protein
   b. Protein
   c. Amino acids

d. Cholesterol

66. Substance produced by the liver and found in plant and animal fats that can produce fatty deposits or atherosclerotic plaques in the blood vessel is called?
    a. Organic protein
    b. Protein
    c. Amino acids
    d. Cholesterol

67. A disease in which the body is unable to use glucose for energy as a result of either a lack of insulin production in the pancreas or resistance to insulin on the cellular level is?
    a. Diverticulosis
    b. Diabetes mellitus type 3
    c. Diabetes mellitus type 2
    d. Diabetes mellitus type 1

68. Presence of pouchlike herniations through the muscular layer of the colon is?
    a. Diverticulosis
    b. Diabetes mellitus type 3
    c. Diabetes mellitus type 2
    d. Diabetes mellitus type 1

69. A disease in which beta cells in the pancreas no longer produce insulin is?

a. Diverticulosis
b. Diabetes mellitus type 3
c. Diabetes mellitus type 2
d. Diabetes mellitus type 1

70. Compounds with at least one unpaired electron that makes the compound unstable and highly reactive is?
    a. Hydrogenation
    b. Free radicals
    c. Digestion
    d. Psyllium

71. Process of converting food into chemical substances that can be used by the body is?
    a. Hydrogenation
    b. Free radicals
    c. Digestion
    d. Psyllium

72. Grain that is found in some cereal products, in certain dietary supplements and in certain bulk fiber laxatives is called?
    a. Turgor
    b. Free radicals
    c. Vertigo
    d. Psyllium

73. A sensation of faintness or an inability to maintain normal balance is called?

a. Turgor
b. Free radicals
c. Vertigo
d. Psyllium

74. Resistance of the skin to being grasped between the fingers and released is?
    a. Turgor
    b. Free radicals
    c. Vertigo
    d. Psyllium

75. Which of the following is not a vital sign?
    a. Temprature
    b. BMI
    c. Blood pressure
    d. Respiration

76. The balance between the heat loss and the heat produced is called?
    a. Heat waves
    b. Metabolism
    c. Body Temperature
    d. All of the above

77. Which of this is not a factor that affects body temperature?
    a. Age
    b. Stress

c. Physical activity

d. Sleep

78. Abnormal prolonged and deep breathing usually associated with acute anxiety or emotional tension is called?

　　a. Hyperventilation

　　b. Hypothermia

　　c. Hypoventilation

　　d. Afebrile

79. Blood pressure below normal is?

　　a. Hypertension

　　b. Hypotension

　　c. Febrile

　　d. Afebrile

80. _____ Is the term used when having normal body temperature.

　　a. Hyperpyrexia

　　b. Hypothermia

　　c. Febrile

　　d. Afebrile

81. Fluctuating fever that returns to or below baseline, then rises again is called?

　　a. Intermittent

　　b. Remittent

　　c. Continuous

　　d. Recurrent

185

82. Fever that remains fairly constant above the baseline; and does not fluctuate is called?
   a. Intermittent
   b. Remittent
   c. Continuous
   d. Recurrent

83. _____ temperature is considered by the majority of the physicians as the most accurate method of temperature measurement
   a. Rectal
   b. Axillary
   c. Tympanic temperature
   d. Oral

84. _____ is useful for children and confused patients because of the speed of operation?
   a. Rectal
   b. Digital
   c. Tympanic temperature
   d. Oral

85. _____ is pertaining to an elevated blood pressure?
   a. Hyperpyrexia
   b. Hypothermia
   c. Febrile
   d. Afebrile

86. The _____ is frequently used in emergencies and to check the pulse during CPR?
    a. Radial
    b. Temporal
    c. Carotid
    d. Apical

87. The _____ is often used for infants and young children if the radial pulse is difficult to feel or irregular?
    a. Radial
    b. Temporal
    c. Carotid
    d. Apical

88. The normal adult pulse rate ranges between _____ beat per minute?
    a. 80-120
    b. 60-100
    c. 65-95
    d. 90-110

89. The site most commonly used for taking pulse is called?
    a. Radial artery
    b. Apical pulse
    c. Brachial pulse

d. Femoral pulse

90. When measuring a pulse, the following characteristics are taken into account except?
    a. Volume
    b. Length
    c. Rate
    d. Rhythm

91. _____ is a measure of the number of heartbeats felt from the movement of blood through the artery?
    a. Volume
    b. Length
    c. Rate
    d. Rhythm

92. The time between each pulse beat is called?
    a. Volume
    b. Length
    c. Rate
    d. Rhythm

93. _____ reflects the strength of the heart when it contracts?
    a. Volume
    b. Length
    c. Rate
    d. Rhythm

94. The normal adult pulse rate ranges between
    _____ beat per minute?
    a. 80-120
    b. 60-100
    c. 65-95
    d. 75-110

95. The normal 7-11years pulse rate ranges between
    _____ beat per minute?
    a. 80-120
    b. 60-100
    c. 65-95
    d. 75-110

96. Which of these is not a blood pressure reading?
    a. Systolic
    b. Diastolic
    c. Pulse pressure
    d. None of the above

97. The lowest pressure level that occurs when the heart is relaxed and no pulse beat is felt is called?
    a. Systolic
    b. Diastolic
    c. Pulse pressure
    d. Blood pressure

98. The highest pressure level that occurs when the heart is contracting and the pulse beat is felt is called?
    a. Systolic
    b. Diastolic
    c. Pulse pressure
    d. Blood pressure

99. As a medical assistance it is necessary to tell a patient that you will be counting their respiration?
    a. True
    b. False
    c. It depends
    d. None of the above

100. When measuring respiration, the following characteristics are taken into account except?
    a. Length
    b. Rate
    c. Depth
    d. Rhythm

101. _____ is the reflection of the pressure of blood against the walls of the arteries?
    a. Systolic
    b. Diastolic

c. Pulse pressure

d. Blood pressure

102.   The difference between systolic and diastolic pressure is?

    a. Heart rate

    b. Blood pressure

    c. Pulse pressure

    d. Contraction

103.   The instrument used to measure blood pressure is called?

    a. Manometer

    b. Sphygmomanometer

    c. Thermometer

    d. Anthropometry

104.   The science that deals with the measurement of the size, weight and proportions of the human body is?

    a. Manometer

    b. Sphygmomanometer

    c. Thermometer

    d. Anthropometry

105.   Respirations that are regular in rhythm but slower than normal in rate is?

    a. Bradypnea

    b. Bradycardia

    c. Dyspnea

d. Hyperpnea

106. A slow heartbeat; a pulse below 60 beats per minutes is called?
   a. Bradypnea
   b. Bradycardia
   c. Dyspnea
   d. Hyperpnea

107. Increase in depth of breathing is called?
   a. Bradypnea
   b. Bradycardia
   c. Dyspnea
   d. Hyperpnea

108. Difficult or painful breathing is?
   a. Bradypnea
   b. Bradycardia
   c. Dyspnea
   d. Hyperpnea

109. Irregular heart rhythm is called?
   a. Irrhythm
   b. Arrhythmia
   c. Diurnal rhythm
   d. Bounding

110. A waxy secretion in the ear canal is?
   a. Cerumen
   b. Thready

c. Syncope

d. Peripheral

111. _____ is pertaining to an area that is outside or away from an organ or structure?

a. Cerumen

b. Thready

c. Syncope

d. Peripheral

112. _____ describes a pulse that is scarcely perceptible?

a. Cerumen

b. Thready

c. Syncope

d. Peripheral

113. A brief lapse of consciousness is known as?

a. Cerumen

b. Thready

c. Syncope

d. Peripheral

114. Respirations that are rapid and shallow is called?

a. Tachycardia

b. Tachypnea

c. Otitis externa

d. Orthopnea

115.　　Condition in which individual must sit or stand to breath comfortably is?
   a. Tachycardia
   b. Tachypnea
   c. Otitis externa
   d. Orthopnea

116.　　Inflammation or infection of the external auditory carnal is called?
   a. Tachycardia
   b. Tachypnea
   c. Otitis externa
   d. Orthopnea

117.　　Rapid but regular heart rate exceeding 100 beats per minute is called?
   a. Tachycardia
   b. Tachypnea
   c. Otitis externa
   d. Orthopnea

118.　　Abnormal sound or murmur heard on auscultation of an organ, vessel or gland is?
   a. Rales
   b. Clubbing
   c. Bruit
   d. Rhonchi

119.   Abnormal or cracking breathing sounds during inspiration is called?
   a. Rales
   b. Clubbing
   c. Bruit
   d. Rhonchi

120.   Abnormal Rumbling sounds on expiration that indicate airway obstruction by thick secretions or spasms is?
   a. Rales
   b. Clubbing
   c. Bruit
   d. Rhonchi

121.   An Abnormal enlargement of the fingertips usually seen with advanced heart and lungs disease is?
   a. Rales
   b. Clubbing
   c. Bruit
   d. Rhonchi

122.   White part of the eye that forms the orbit is called?
   a. Sclera
   b. Pupil
   c. Murmur

d. Peristalsis

123.   Rhythmic contraction of involuntary muscles lining the gastrointestinal tract is called?
    a. Sclera
    b. Pupil
    c. Murmur
    d. Peristalsis

124.   Abnormal sound heard when auscultating the heart that may or may not have a pathologic origin is called?
    a. Sclera
    b. Pupil
    c. Murmur
    d. Peristalsis

125.   Inspection of a cavity or organ by passing light through its wall is called?
    a. Transillumination
    b. Vasoconstriction
    c. Nodules
    d. Intercellular

126.   Contraction of the muscles lining blood vessels that results in decreased lumen size is called?
    a. Transillumination
    b. Vasoconstriction

c. Nodules

d. Intercellular

127. Small lumps, lesions, or swellings felt when palpating the skin is called?
   a. Transillumination
   b. Vasoconstriction
   c. Nodules
   d. Intercellular

128. _____ is the study of body functions?
   a. Anatomy
   b. Human science
   c. Cell
   d. Physiology

129. The study of how body is shaped and structured is called?
   a. Anatomy
   b. Human science
   c. Cell
   d. Physiology

130. Which of the following is not a part of the cell?
   a. Plasma
   b. Tissues
   c. Cytoplasm
   d. Nucleus

131.　　When cells are similar in structure and are placed together they form?
   a. Organs
   b. Tissues
   c. Systems
   d. Cells

132.　　_____ is composed of several organs and their associated structure?
   a. Organs
   b. Tissues
   c. Systems
   d. Cells

133.　　_____ is composed of two or more types of tissue bound together to form a more complex structure for a common purpose or function?
   a. Organs
   b. Tissues
   c. Systems
   d. Cells

134.　　In the physical examination of a patient, who is responsible for making sure that the room is ready and prepared?
   a. Physician
   b. Janitor

c. Medical Assistant

d. All of the above

135.   In the preparation of the exam room the area should be checked at the beginning and end of the day?

a. True

b. False

c. Maybe

d. None of the above

136.   The following instrument are needed for physical examination except?

a. Turning folk

b. Tape measure

c. Reflex hammer

d. None of the above

137.   The device used when auscultating certain areas of the body is called?

a. Percussion hammer

b. Stethoscope

c. Ophthalmoscope

d. Otoscope

138.   _____ is used to inspect the inner structure of the eye?

a. Percussion hammer

b. Stethoscope

c. Ophthalmoscope

d. Otoscope

139. _____ is used to examine the external auditory canal and tympanic membrane?
   a. Percussion hammer
   b. Stethoscope
   c. Ophthalmoscope
   d. Otoscope

140. Which of the following is also called Reflex hammer?
   a. Percussion hammer
   b. Stethoscope
   c. Ophthalmoscope
   d. Otoscope

141. Which of the following is not a method of examination for a complete physical examination?
   a. Inspection
   b. Palpation
   c. Mensuration
   d. None of the above

142. Listening to sounds produced by internal organs usually done to evaluate the heart, lungs, and the abdomen is?
   a. Auscultation
   b. Percussion

c. Palpation

d. Manipulation

143.   Which of the following is not a position for the physical examination of a patient?

a. Percussion

b. Lithotomy

c. Semi-fowler

d. None of the above

144.   _____ position is used for rectal and vaginal examinations and as treatment to bring uterus to normal position?

a. Sim's

b. Trendelenburg

c. Knee-chest

d. Fowler's

145.   Which of this is not the Medical Assistant's role in the physical examination?

a. Room preparation

b. Patient preparation

c. Assisting the physician

d. None of the above

146.   The inability to speak because of a loss of voice is?

a. Aphasia

b. Aphonia

c. Dysphasia

d. Motor aphasia

147. When a patient knows what he want s to say but cannot use muscles properly to speak is called?

    a. Aphasia

    b. Aphonia

    c. Dysphasia

    d. Motor aphasia

148. The loss of expression by speech or writing because of an injury or disease of the brain center?

    a. Aphasia

    b. Aphonia

    c. Dysphasia

    d. Motor aphasia

149. A lack of coordination and failure to arrange words in proper order usually caused by a brain lesion is?

    a. Aphasia

    b. Aphonia

    c. Dysphasia

    d. Motor aphasia

150. Skin turgor is checked by pinching the posterior surface of the hand; a delay in the return of the skin indicates?

a. Hydration
b. Good skin
c. Dehydration
d. None of the above

151.   Which of the following is not a type of tissue in the body?
a. Nucleus
b. Epithelial
c. Connective
d. Muscular

152.   _____ is the study of the biologic effects of a drug on a patient when used as a medical treatment and the actions of a drug in the body overtime?
a. Chemistry
b. Biology
c. Clinical Pharmacology
d. Ecology

153.   Pharmaceutical companies developing new medications must first gain approval from?
a. WHO
b. HIPAA
c. DEA
d. FDA

154.   The _____ was established in 1973 as part of the department of justice to enforce federal law regarding the use of illegal drugs?
   a. WHO
   b. HIPAA
   c. DEA
   d. FDA

155.   _____ is the improper use of common drugs that can lead to dependence or toxicity?
   a. Drug dependency
   b. Drug misuse
   c. Psychologic dependency
   d. Drug abuse

156.   The continuous or periodic self-administration of a drug that could result in addiction is called?
   a. Drug dependency
   b. Drug misuse
   c. Psychologic dependency
   d. Drug abuse

157.   The inability to function unless under the influence of a substance is called?
   a. Drug dependency
   b. Drug misuse
   c. Psychologic dependency

d. Drug abuse

158. The compulsory craving for the effects of a substance is?
   a. Drug dependency
   b. Drug misuse
   c. Psychologic dependency
   d. Drug abuse

159. _____ is the study of the movement of drugs throughout the body is called?
   a. Pharmacology
   b. Pharmovement
   c. Pharmacokinetics
   d. Pharmbody

160. Liquid oral medications are dissolved more rapidly than solid form because they do not have to be dissolved by _____?
   a. Mouth
   b. Liver
   c. Intestine
   d. Gastrointestinal fluids

161. Although injection of medication leads to rapid absorption it could increase the danger of?
   a. Wounds

b. Infection

c. Restriction

d. None of the above

162. The generic name for "Amoxicillin" is?
   a. Amlodipine
   b. Metoprolol
   c. Amoxicillin
   d. Azithromycin

163. The generic name for "Zyrtec" is?
   a. Amlodipine
   b. Cetirizine
   c. Amoxicillin
   d. Zyrtec

164. The classification of use of "Lorazepam" is for?
   a. Antianxiety
   b. Thyroid hormone replacement
   c. Analgesic
   d. Lipid lowering agent

165. The classification of use of "Levothyroxine" is for?
   a. Antianxiety
   b. Thyroid hormone replacement
   c. Analgesic
   d. Lipid lowering agent

166. The classification of use of "ibuprofen" is for?
a. Antiplatelet agent
b. Thyroid hormone replacement
c. Analgesic
d. Nonsteroidal antiflammatory agent

167. The classification of use of "Sertraline" is for?
a. Antianxiety
b. Thyroid hormone replacement
c. Analgesic
d. Antidepressant

168. The classification of use of "Simvastatin" is for?
a. Antianxiety
b. Thyroid hormone replacement
c. Analgesic
d. Lipid lowering agent

169. The generic name for "Toprol-XL" is?
a. Amlodipine
b. Metoprolol
c. Amoxicillin
d. Azithromycin

170. The generic name for "Zantac" is?
a. Amlodipine

b. Metoprolol

c. Ranitidine HCI

d. Azithromycin

171.   The generic name for "Norvasc" is?
   a. Amlodipine
   b. Metoprolol
   c. Ranitidine HCI
   d. Azithromycin

172.   The generic name for "Zithromax" is?
   a. Amlodipine
   b. Metoprolol
   c. Ranitidine HCI
   d. Azithromycin

173.   Which of this is not a part of a prescription?
   a. Subscription
   b. Inscription
   c. Side effect
   d. Refill information

174.   _____ refers to the administration of drugs by injection?
   a. Therapeutic range
   b. Parenteral
   c. Lumen
   d. Injection

175. Blood concentration of a drug that produces the desired effect without toxicity is called?
    a. Therapeutic range
    b. Parenteral
    c. Lumen
    d. Injection

176. Space within a vessel or tube is called?
    a. Therapeutic range
    b. Parenteral
    c. Lumen
    d. Injection

177. The _____ route of administering drugs by injection is chosen in an emergency for fast action or when larger amounts of medication must be absorbed?
    a. Subcutaneous
    b. Intravenous
    c. Intraspinal
    d. Intramuscular

178. The _____ injects medication directly into the vein?
    a. Subcutaneous
    b. Intravenous
    c. Intraspinal
    d. Intramuscular

179.   The _____ route of administering drugs by injection is chosen when a slower, prolonged effect is desired?
    a. Subcutaneous
    b. Intravenous
    c. Intraspinal
    d. Intramuscular

180.   Which of this is not the Medical Assistant's role in the Hospital?
    a. Room preparation
    b. Patient preparation
    c. Assisting the physician
    d. Administration of IV medication to patients

181.   The application of medication to the skin, eye and ears is called?
    a. Mucous membrane absorption
    b. Topical absorption
    c. External absorption
    d. All of the above

182.   The placenta has no method for blocking substance so whatever the mother consumes is passed through the placenta to the developing fetus?
    a. True
    b. False

c. At times

d. None of the above

183. The _____ are the most important route for the elimination of drugs?

    a. Sweat glands

    b. Saliva

    c. Skin

    d. Kidney

184. Patient taking multiple medications may increase the risk for liver-related problems with metabolism?

    a. True

    b. False

    c. At times

    d. None of the above

185. During metabolism, drugs are converted into harmful byproducts?

    a. True

    b. False

    c. At times

    d. None of the above

186. The amount of time it takes for half a dose of medication to be excreted from the body is called?

    a. Waiting period

    b. Pending time

c. Half life

d. Awaiting time

187.   Which of this is not a factor that affects drug action?

a. Sex

b. Time of the day

c. Body weight

d. None of the above

188.   Which of these age groups are sensitive to drugs because it could affect their central nervous system?

a. Newborns

b. Elderly individuals

c. None of the above

d. All of the above

189.   Intramuscular medications are more absorbed faster in women than men?

a. True

b. False

c. At times

d. None of the above

190.   A patient's personality can never affect whether he or she will be cooperative in following directions for a particular drugs, likewise his negative mind set or mental attitude cannot reduce an expected response to a drug?

a. True
b. False
c. At times
d. None of the above

191. _____ occurs when a patient acquires a tolerance to one drug and becomes resistance to other similar drugs?
   a. Acquired tolerance
   b. Physical dependency
   c. Cross-tolerance
   d. Non forbearance

192. Which of the following drugs classification decreases the acidity in the stomach?
   a. Antibiotics
   b. Antacids
   c. Analgesics
   d. Adrenergic blocking agents

193. Which of the following drugs classification lessens the sensory function of the brain and also blocks pain receptors?
   a. Antibiotics
   b. Antacids
   c. Analgesics
   d. Adrenergic blocking agents

194. Which of the following drugs classification delays or blocks the clotting of blood?
   a. Anticoagulant
   b. Anticonvulsants
   c. Antipruritics
   d. Antineoplastic

195. Which of the following drugs classification inhibits the development of and destroys cancerous cells?
   a. Anticoagulant
   b. Anticonvulsants
   c. Antipruritics
   d. Antineoplastic

196. Which of the following drugs classification relieves itching?
   a. Anticoagulant
   b. Anticonvulsants
   c. Antipruritics
   d. Antineoplastic

197. Which of the following drugs classification inhibits the cough center?
   a. Antipyretics
   b. Antispasmodics
   c. Antitussives
   d. Decongestant

198.　Which of the following drugs classification relieves local congestion in the tissue?
   a. Antipyretics
   b. Antispasmodics
   c. Antitussives
   d. Decongestant

199.　Which of the following drugs classification reduces body temperature?
   a. Antipyretics
   b. Antispasmodics
   c. Antitussives
   d. Decongestant

200.　Which of the following drug classification induces sleep and lessen the activity of the brain?
   a. Miotics
   b. Narcotics
   c. Hypnotics
   d. Hemostatics agent

201.　Which of the following drug classification Controls bleeding?
   a. Miotics
   b. Narcotics
   c. Hypnotics
   d. Hemostatics agents

202. Which of the following drug classification depresses the CNS and causes insensibility and stupor?
   a. Miotics
   b. Narcotics
   c. Hypnotics
   d. Mydriatics

203. Which of the following drug classification causes the pupil of the eye to contract
   a. Miotics
   b. Narcotics
   c. Hypnotics
   d. Mydriatics

204. The following are system of measurement for medication except?
   a. Standard system
   b. Metric system
   c. Apothecary system
   d. Household system

205. Which of this system of measurement are not precisely accurate?
   a. Standard system
   b. Metric system
   c. Apothecary system
   d. Household system

206. In which of this system of measurement is a decimal based on the number 10?
    a. Standard system
    b. Metric system
    c. Apothecary system
    d. Household system

207. Which of this system of measurement is "grain" a basic unit of weight for a solid medication?
    a. Standard system
    b. Metric system
    c. Apothecary system
    d. Household system

208. Which of this system of measurement is "pound" (lb) the basic unit of weight for a solid medication?
    a. Standard system
    b. Metric system
    c. Apothecary system
    d. Household system

209. Which of this system of measurement is "minim" a basic unit of volume for a liquid medication?
    a. Standard system
    b. Metric system
    c. Apothecary system

d. Household system

210. The following are method for verifying the accuracy of calculations by the medical assistance except?
   a. Verify the system of measurement
   b. Checking patients to see if he has any symptoms
   c. Check calculations for accuracy
   d. None of the above

211. The following are rights for proper drug administration in safeguarding the patient?
   a. Right route
   b. Right dose
   c. Right space
   d. Right drug

212. Tablets are sugar-coated to?
   a. Taste better
   b. Protect stomach mucosa
   c. Prevent stomach irritation
   d. Prevent vomiting

213. Tablets are enteric-coated to?
   a. Taste better
   b. Protect stomach mucosa
   c. Prevent stomach irritation
   d. Prevent vomiting

214.   Buffered tablets are designed to?
    a. Taste better
    b. Protect stomach mucosa
    c. Prevent stomach irritation
    d. Prevent vomiting

215.   Which of the following size of needle is used for intradermal injections?
    a. 14-16
    b. 20-24
    c. 25-26
    d. 27-28

216.   _____ is considered as the safest IM injection site for infants?
    a. Deltoid site
    b. Vastus Lateralis site
    c. Ventrogluteal site
    d. Arm site

217.   When vastus lateralis site is used in an adult the needle should be injected at _____ degree angle?
    a. 45
    b. 60
    c. 90
    d. 180

218.   When vastus lateralis site is used for infant and children the needle should be injected at _____ degree angle?

   a. 25
   b. 45
   c. 60
   d. 90

219.   _____is defined as the immediate care given to a person who has been injured or has suddenly taken ill?

   a. First aid
   b. Primary care
   c. Immediate care
   d. Emergency

220.   Rapid, random, ineffective contractions of the heart is called

   a. Defibrillation
   b. Fibrillation
   c. Hematuria
   d. Idiopathic

221.   Blood in the urine is called?

   a. Defibrillation
   b. Fibrillation
   c. Hematuria
   d. Idiopathic

222. _____ is pertaining to no known cause of a condition or disease?
   a. Defibrillation
   b. Fibrillation
   c. Hematuria
   d. Idiopathic

223. The following are automated external defibrillation precautions except?
   a. All cloths should be removed
   b. A patient who wears glasses can leave his glasses on to see
   c. The patient must be lying on a dry surface
   d. None of the above

224. _____ is the smallest yet most detailed and complex organ of the body?
   a. Cell
   b. Organ
   c. Eye
   d. Tissue

225. Which of the following is not a refractive error?
   a. Hyperopia
   b. Astigmatism
   c. Strabismus
   d. Myopia

226.   Failure of both eyes to look in the same direction at the same time is?
   a. Hyperopia
   b. Astigmatism
   c. Strabismus
   d. Myopia

227.   When light rays entering the eye focus in front of the retina causing objects at a distance to appear blurry and dull is?
   a. Hyperopia
   b. Astigmatism
   c. Strabismus
   d. Myopia

228.   When light enters the eye and focuses behind the retina, the person has?
   a. Hyperopia
   b. Astigmatism
   c. Strabismus
   d. Myopia

229.   Inflammation of the glands and lash follicles along the margins of the eyelids with symptoms like itching along the eyelash margin is?
   a. Blepharitis
   b. Keratitis

c. Hordeolum

d. Conjunctivitis

230. A localized purulent infection of a sebaceous gland of the eyelid where the area is inflamed, swollen and painful is called?

a. Blepharitis

b. Keratitis

c. Hordeolum

d. Conjunctivitis

231. Inflammation of the cornea of the eye resulting in superficial ulcerations is?

a. Blepharitis

b. Keratitis

c. Hordeolum

d. Conjunctivitis

232. The following are disorders of the eyeball except?

a. Cataract

b. Vitreous humor

c. Glaucoma

d. Macular Degeneration

233. Anatomically the organ of hearing is divided into 3 sections, which of this is not a section?

a. Outer Ear

b. Middle Ear

c. Frontal Ear

d. Inner Ear

234. The _____ test is used if the patient reports hearing is better in one ear than in the other?

a. Rinne

b. Weber

c. Audiometric

d. None of the above

235. The _____ test is designed to compare air conduction sound with bone conduction sound?

a. Rinne

b. Weber

c. Audiometric

d. None of the above

236. Yellow discoloration of the skin and mucus membrane resulting from deposits of bile pigment because of excess bilirubin in the blood is?

a. Leukoderma

b. Ecchymosis

c. Jaundice

d. Alopecia

237. Lack of skin pigmentation especially in patches is?
   a. Leukoderma
   b. Ecchymosis
   c. Jaundice
   d. Alopecia

238. Bluish-black skin discoloration produced by hemorrhagic areas is?
   a. Leukoderma
   b. Ecchymosis
   c. Jaundice
   d. Alopecia

239. Partial or complete lack of hair is?
   a. Leukoderma
   b. Ecchymosis
   c. Jaundice
   d. Alopecia

240. Causes of herniation include the following except?
   a. Congenital weakness of the structures
   b. Trauma
   c. Increased upward pressure from the abdomen
   d. Dizziness

241. _____ occurs when the gastroesophageal sphincter at the distal end of

the esophagus does not close properly, allowing acidic stomach content to leak back or reflux into the esophagus?
a. Hernia
b. GERD
c. Ulcer
d. Opened Esophagus

242. _____ is the narrowing and hardening of the pyloric sphincter at the distal end of the stomach, apparent in first born newborn males between 2-6 weeks?
a. Food poisoning
b. Peptic ulcer
c. Pyloric poisoning
d. Pyloric stenosis

243. The study of the urinary tract in both male and female is called?
a. Anatomy
b. Urology
c. Urinary study
d. Physiology

244. Men are more susceptible to urinary tract infection than men?
a. True
b. False
c. Maybe

d. None of the above

245.　　Sudden, compelling desire to urinate and the inability to control the release of urine is?
   a. Urgency
   b. Urinating
   c. Erythropoietin
   d. Copulation

246.　　Which of the following is also known as sexual intercourse?
   a. Urgency
   b. Urinating
   c. Erythropoietin
   d. Copulation

247.　　The branch of medicine that deals with diseases of the genital tract in women is called?
   a. Genitology
   b. Obstetrics
   c. Gynecology
   d. Anatology

248.　　The branch of medicine that deals with pregnancy, labor and postnatal period is?
   a. Genitology
   b. Obstetrics
   c. Gynecology
   d. Anatology

249.   The absence of mensuration for a minimum of 6 months?
   a. Menorrhagia
   b. Metrorrhagia
   c. Amenorrhea
   d. Endometrics

250.   Excessive menstrual blood loss lasting longer than 7 days is called?
   a. Menorrhagia
   b. Metrorrhagia
   c. Amenorrhea
   d. Endometrics

MA Test 3	
1	C
2	D
3	B
4	C
5	D
6	C
7	A
8	C
9	B
10	A
11	B
12	A
13	C
14	B
15	D
16	D
17	B
18	A
19	C
20	B
21	A
22	C
23	B
24	B
25	C
26	D
27	A
28	B
29	C

30	D
31	A
32	C
33	B
34	C
35	D
36	B
37	C
38	A
39	B
40	B
41	C
42	D
43	D
44	D
45	D
46	A
47	B
48	D
49	D
50	C
51	C
52	A
53	B
54	A
55	B
56	B
57	C
58	D
59	C
60	A
61	C

62	D
63	A
64	C
65	C
66	D
67	C
68	A
69	D
70	B
71	C
72	D
73	C
74	A
75	B
76	C
77	D
78	A
79	B
80	D
81	A
82	C
83	A
84	C
85	C
86	C
87	D
88	B
89	A
90	B
91	C
92	D
93	A

94	B
95	D
96	C
97	B
98	A
99	B
100	A
101	D
102	C
103	B
104	D
105	A
106	B
107	D
108	C
109	B
110	A
111	D
112	B
113	C
114	B
115	D
116	C
117	A
118	C
119	A
120	D
121	B
122	A
123	D
124	C
125	A

126	B
127	C
128	D
129	A
130	B
131	B
132	C
133	A
134	C
135	B
136	D
137	B
138	C
139	D
140	A
141	D
142	A
143	A
144	C
145	D
146	B
147	D
148	A
149	C
150	C
151	A
152	C
153	D
154	C
155	C
156	D
157	A

158	C
159	C
160	D
161	B
162	C
163	B
164	A
165	B
166	D
167	D
168	D
169	B
170	C
171	A
172	D
173	C
174	B
175	A
176	C
177	D
178	B
179	A
180	D
181	B
182	A
183	D
184	A
185	B
186	C
187	D
188	D
189	B

190	B
191	C
192	B
193	C
194	C
195	D
196	C
197	C
198	D
199	A
200	C
201	D
202	B
203	A
204	A
205	D
206	B
207	C
208	D
209	C
210	B
211	C
212	A
213	B
214	C
215	D
216	B
217	C
218	B
219	A
220	B
221	C

222	D
223	B
224	C
225	C
226	C
227	D
228	A
229	A
230	C
231	B
232	B
233	C
234	B
235	A
236	C
237	A
238	B
239	D
240	D
241	B
242	D
243	B
244	B
245	A
246	D
247	C
248	B
249	C
250	A

Test 4

1. The age range of pediatric patient is from?
    a. 2-5 years
    b. Newborn – 10 years
    c. Birth – Puberty
    d. 1 – 20 years

2. Pediatric care starts from?
    a. When the child is born
    b. Before the child is born
    c. 1st week of life
    d. All of the above

3. _____ considers qualitative maturation in motor, mental social and language skills?
    a. Growth
    b. Progression
    c. Development
    d. Change

4. _____ refers to measureable changes such as height and weight?
    a. Growth
    b. Progression
    c. Development

d. Change

5. The growth pattern of an average baby's birth weight doubles at?
    a. 3 months
    b. 6 months
    c. 12 months
    d. 1 year and half

6. The assessment of the Denver II developmental screening test focuses on the following development areas except?
    a. Language
    b. Personal skill
    c. Sleeping ability
    d. Fine motor skill

7. Which of the following causes an infant between the ages of 2 weeks to 4months to draw up legs, clench fist and cry inconsolably?
    a. Diarrhea
    b. Common cold
    c. Conjunctivitis
    d. Colic

8. A viral inflammation of the larynx and trachea that causes edema and spasm of the cords is called?

a. Asthma

b. Bronchiolitis

c. Croup

d. Tonsillitis

9. A viral infection of the small bronchi and bronchioles that usually affects children under 3 years of age is?

a. Asthma

b. Bronchiolitis

c. Croup

d. Tonsillitis

10. Which of the following is also called "Pinkeye"?

a. Meningitis

b. Varicella

c. Fifth disease

d. Conjunctivitis

11. Which of the following is also called "erythema infectiosum"?

a. Meningitis

b. Varicella

c. Fifth disease

d. Conjunctivitis

12. _____ is caused by white or yellowish pus that may cause the eyelids to stick shut in the morning?
    a. Meningitis
    b. Varicella
    c. Fifth disease
    d. Conjunctivitis

13. _____ is an inflammation of the membranes that cover the brain and spinal cord?
    a. Meningitis
    b. Varicella
    c. Fifth disease
    d. Conjunctivitis

14. Which of the following has a symptom of salty taste to the skin, large greasy foul-smelling stools, abdominal distention, chronic cough and frequent respiratory infection?
    a. Cystic fibrosis
    b. Hepatitis B
    c. Reye's syndrome
    d. Varicella

15. Which of the following is an inherited disorder?
    a. Cystic fibrosis

b. Hepatitis B

c. Reye's syndrome

d. Varicella

16. A child who is allergic to egg can receive all the following vaccines except?

    a. Varicella

    b. Measles

    c. Mumps

    d. None of the above

17. The Apgar score evaluates an infant's physical condition at what time after birth?

    a. 1 and 5 minutes

    b. 5 and 10 minutes

    c. After the child is being fed

    d. At the first pediatrician visit

18. Which of the following is not a role of the medical assistant in pediatric procedure?

    a. Measuring and weighing children

    b. Performing hemoglobin checks

    c. Administering immunization

    d. None of the above

19. Doctors that treat the body from the view point that the body can heal itself when the skeletal system is in proper alignment is?

a. Chiropractor
b. Osteopaths
c. Rheumatologist
d. Orthopedic physician

20._____ are specialist in treating inflammatory joint disorder?
   a. Chiropractor
   b. Osteopaths
   c. Rheumatologist
   d. Orthopedic physician

21. The _____ diagnoses and treats diseases and disorders of the musculoskeletal system and deals primarily with bones?
   a. Chiropractor
   b. Osteopaths
   c. Rheumatologist
   d. Orthopedic physician

22. Tough connective tissue bands that hold joints together by attaching to the bones on either side of a joint is?
   a. Ligament
   b. Tendons
   c. Cartilage
   d. Veins

23. Tough bands of connective tissue connecting muscles to bones is called?
    a. Ligament
    b. Tendons
    c. Cartilage
    d. Veins

24. Rubbery, smooth somewhat elastic connective tissue covering the end of bones is?
    a. Ligament
    b. Tendons
    c. Cartilage
    d. Veins

25. Instrument for measuring the degree of motion in a joint is?
    a. Jointometer
    b. Goniometer
    c. Motiometer
    d. None of the above

26. End of a long bone is?
    a. Epiphysis
    b. Diaphysis
    c. Midphysis
    d. Endpysis

27. Midportion of a long bone that contains medullary cavity is?
    a. Epiphysis
    b. Diaphysis
    c. Midphysis
    d. Endpysis

28. Which of these muscles are voluntary and can be controlled when they contract or relax?
    a. Cardiac
    b. Smooth
    c. Skeletal
    d. None of the above

29. What is the Muscle action for the description "movement away from the midline"?
    a. Abduction
    b. Abortion
    c. Adduction
    d. Aligning

30. What is the Muscle action for the description "movement towards the midline"?
    a. Abduction
    b. Abortion
    c. Adduction
    d. Aligning

31. What is the Muscle action for the description "raising the foot"?
    a. Flexion
    b. Plantar flexion
    c. Dorsiflexion
    d. Pronation

32. What is the Muscle action for the description "lowering the foot"?
    a. Flexion
    b. Plantar flexion
    c. Dorsiflexion
    d. Pronation

33. What type of fracture is it when the bone is cracked on one side and intact on the other side because of softness?
    a. Pathologic
    b. Salter-Harris
    c. Impacted
    d. Greenstick

34. What type of fracture is it when the bone is broken and the ends are driven into each other?
    a. Pathologic
    b. Salter-Harris

c. Impacted

d. Greenstick

35._____ is a type of fracture that occurs spontaneously as a result of disease.

    a. Pathologic

    b. Salter-Harris

    c. Impacted

    d. Greenstick

36._____ are fibrous sacs that lie between tendons and bones?

    a. Ligament

    b. Bursae

    c. Cartilage

    d. Veins

37. Which of the following is not a muscular disorder?

    a. Gout

    b. Fractures

    c. Dislocation

    d. None of the above

38. Which of these has a symptom of painful joint that is out of place and has severely decreased ROM?

    a. Gout

b. Fractures

c. Dislocation

d. None of the above

39. Which of these signs and symptoms has a painful inflamed joint, often affects great toe and very sensitive to touch and movement?

    a. Gout

    b. Fractures

    c. Dislocation

    d. None of the above

40. Which of the below signs and symptoms does not require Analgesics and NSAIDs as its treatment and medication?

    a. Gout

    b. Fractures

    c. Dislocation

    d. None of the above

41. _____ is a wrenching or twisting of a joint in an abnormal plane of motion or beyond its normal ROM that results in the stretching and/or tearing of a ligament?

    a. Strain

    b. Sprain

    c. Dislocation

d. Fracture

42._____ is a simple overstretching of a muscle or tendon and can be caused by a partial complete tear of tissue?
   a. Strain
   b. Sprain
   c. Dislocation
   d. Fracture

43._____ is a break or crack in a bone that generally is the result of a trauma or disease?
   a. Strain
   b. Sprain
   c. Dislocation
   d. Fracture

44. Which of the following is not a skeletal disorder?
   a. Osteoporosis
   b. Fracture
   c. Herniated Disk
   d. None of the above

45._____ occurs spontaneously and may persist for hours, they are caused by heavy exercise and muscle fatigue and might be as a result of dehydration, kidney failure etc?

a. Spasm

b. Sprain

c. Fracture

d. None of the above

46. Which of the following is not a medical assistant role with orthopedic procedures?

    a. Asking the patient to qualify the intensity of the pain

    b. Request to treat the patient in the absence of the physician

    c. Offer assistance when escorting the patient to the examination room

    d. Record information about any medication taken

47. Which of these is not an ambulatory device?

    a. Wheelchairs

    b. Canes

    c. Walkers

    d. None of the above

48. A physician who treats behavioral disorders and neurological conditions that affects behavior is?

    a. Neurosurgeon

    b. Neurologist

c. Psychiatrist

d. Psychologist

49. Specialist in the diagnosis and treatment of medical orders and conditions of the nervous system is called?

   a. Neurosurgeon

   b. Neurologist

   c. Psychiatrist

   d. Psychologist

50. _____ provides surgical management and treatment for trauma and other requiring surgeries?

   a. Neurosurgeon

   b. Neurologist

   c. Psychiatrist

   d. Psychologist

51. Supportive cells of the nervous systems are called _____ cells?

   a. Sensory Neuron

   b. Central Nervous

   c. Peripheral Nervous

   d. Neurological

52. Which of the following is not a division of the main areas of the brain?

a. Cerebrum

b. Cerebellum

c. Hypothalamus

d. Brain stem

53. The function of the "Trochlear" is for?

    a. Smell

    b. Tongue movement

    c. Eye movement

    d. Throat

54. Which of the following does not have "eye movement" as a function?

    a. Optic

    b. Oculomotor

    c. Trochlear

    d. Abducent

55. The function of the "Olfactory" is for?

    a. Smell

    b. Tongue movement

    c. Eye movement

    d. Throat

56. Which of the following is not a disease or disorder of the central nervous system?

    a. Cerebrovascular Disease

b. Convulsion Disease

c. Alzheimer Disease

d. Migraine Headaches

57. Which of the following is also called ministrokes?

    a. Cerebrovascular Accident

    b. Transient Ischemic Attacks

    c. Migraine Headaches

    d. Shaken baby syndrome

58. A collection of blood in the space between the dura mater and the arachnoid layers of the head is?

    a. Retinal hemorrhages

    b. Migraine headaches

    c. Concussion

    d. Subdural hematoma

59. Shaken baby syndrome can be caused by all the following except?

    a. Throwing up a baby

    b. Dropping a baby

    c. Burping a baby

    d. Baby falling from a sofa

60. In _____ , transection occurs below the midpoint of the spinal cord?

a. Paraplegia

b. Quadriplegia

c. Midaplegia

d. Hemiplegia

61. In _____ , transection occurs in the upper thoracic or cervical region of the spinal cord?

a. Paraplegia

b. Quadriplegia

c. Midaplegia

d. Hemiplegia

62. Which of the following disease does the symptom include facial twitching, drooping eyelid, excessive tearing of the affected eye, drooping mouth and drooling ear?

a. Bell's palsy

b. Amyotrophic lateral sclerosis

c. Carpal tunnel syndrome

d. Dementia Disease

63. Which of these is not a disease of the peripheral nervous system?

a. Bell's palsy

b. Amyotrophic lateral sclerosis

c. Carpal tunnel syndrome

d. Dementia Disease

64. _____ is a rapidly progressive, destructive, ultimately fatal neurologic disease that destroys the motor neurons that are responsible for voluntary muscle control?
    a. Bell's palsy
    b. Amyotrophic lateral sclerosis
    c. Carpal tunnel syndrome
    d. Dementia Disease

65. Types of depressive disorder includes the following except?
    a. Major depressive
    b. Minor depressive
    c. Dysthymic
    d. Bipolar disorder

66. Which if the following is also called "Manic-depression?
    a. Major depressive
    b. Minor depressive
    c. Dysthymic
    d. Bipolar disorder

67. Which of this depressive disorder does the affected individual cycle through a wide range of moods from extreme highs to extreme lows?

a. Major depressive

b. Minor depressive

c. Dysthymic

d. Bipolar disorder

68. A chronic, severe, and disabling brain disorder with symptoms that include hallucinations and delusions with difficulty speaking, expressing emotions and cognitive deficits is?

a. Anxiety disorder

b. Schizophrenia

c. Depressive disorder

d. Peripheral neuropathy

69. The recording of changes in electrical impulses in various areas of the brain by means of electrodes placed on the scalp is called?

a. Electrodiagram

b. Electroencephalography

c. Electrolyte

d. Electrocardiogram

70. Substance that easily be visualized on an x-ray film is called?

a. Radiopaque

b. Paroxysmal

c. Plaque

d. Electro-diagram

71. Which of the following is pertaining to a sudden recurrent spasm of symptoms?
    a. Radiopaque
    b. Paroxysmal
    c. Plaque
    d. Electro-diagram

72. The suffix "-crine" means?
    a. Hormone
    b. Within
    c. Secrete
    d. Excrete

73. Which of these is not an exocrine gland?
    a. Sweat gland
    b. Salivary gland
    c. Thyroid gland
    d. None of the above

74. _____ is the study of hormones, their receptor cells and the results of hormone action?
    a. Adenohypophysis
    b. Pituitary
    c. Thyroid
    d. Endocrinology

75. When(ADH) vasopressin is not produced or released in sufficient amounts, the patient develops a condition called?
    a. Adenohypophysis
    b. Diabetes insipidus
    c. Growth hormone abnormalities
    d. Hypothyroidism

76. Which of the following is a disease of the anterior pituitary?
    a. Adenohypophysis
    b. Diabetes insipidus
    c. Growth hormone abnormalities
    d. Hypothyroidism

77. Which of the following is a disorder of the Thyroid?
    a. Adenohypophysis
    b. Diabetes insipidus
    c. Growth hormone abnormalities
    d. Hypothyroidism

78. A condition in which an individual has a higher than normal blood glucose level but not high enough for a diagnosis of type 2 diabetes is?
    a. Prediabetes
    b. Type 1 diabetes

c. Type 2 diabetes

d. Type 3 diabetes

79. _____ develops in children and young adult and is characterized by a complete absence of insulin production?

   a. Prediabetes

   b. Type 1 diabetes

   c. Type 2 diabetes

   d. Type 3 diabetes

80. _____ develops gradually because of an insufficient amount of insulin and/or resistance at the target cell site or both?

   a. Prediabetes

   b. Type 1 diabetes

   c. Type 2 diabetes

   d. Type 3 diabetes

81. Which of the following has a characteristics where a patient experiences shakiness, vertigo, headache, hunger, fatigue, pallor, confusion, irritability, visual disturbance, seizure and possibly coma?

   a. Hyperglycemia

   b. Hypoglycemia

   c. Hydroglycemia

   d. Polyglycemia

82. Which of the following does the patient experience a sudden onset of polyphagia, polyuria, glycosuria, ketonuria, weight loss, pruritus, fruity breath, dry mouth, nausea, and vomiting?
    a. Hyperglycemia
    b. Hypoglycemia
    c. Hydroglycemia
    d. Polyglycemia

83. Which of this is not a function of the respiratory system?
    a. To store water
    b. Exchange oxygen from the atmosphere for carbon dioxide
    c. To remove metabolic waste
    d. None of the above

84. Every tiny bronchiole terminates into microscopic air called _____ which are made up of thin tissue, which allows the exchange of carbon dioxide through the cell wall?
    a. Bronchioles
    b. Alveoli
    c. Diaphragm

d. Lungs

85. Tiny bronchi are called?
    a. Bronchioles
    b. Alveoli
    c. Diaphragm
    d. Lungs

86. The left bronchus is wider than the right bronchus to accommodate the left bronchus lung lobes which are also wider?
    a. True
    b. False
    c. At times
    d. None of the above

87. _____ transports air from the atmosphere to the lungs?
    a. Rib cage
    b. Upper respiratory tract
    c. Lower respiratory tract
    d. Respiratory alkalosis

88. The thoracic cage is sometimes called the _____?
    a. Rib cage
    b. Upper respiratory tract
    c. Lower respiratory tract

d. Respiratory alkalosis

89. The upper respiratory tract includes the following except?
    a. Nose
    b. Pharynx
    c. Larynx
    d. Lungs

90. _____ is a bony structure that is narrower at the top and wider at the base?
    a. Rib cage
    b. Upper respiratory tract
    c. Lower respiratory tract
    d. Respiratory alkalosis

91. The lower respiratory tract includes the following except?
    a. Trachea
    b. Bronchial tubes
    c. Lungs
    d. Larynx

92. _____ is related to an excess release of carbon dioxide caused by hyperventilation which may be associated with anxiety or acute asthma attack?
    a. Rib cage

b. Upper respiratory tract

c. Lower respiratory tract

d. Respiratory alkalosis

93. The movement of oxygen from the atmosphere into the alveoli is_____?

   a. Inspiration

   b. Expiration

   c. Inhalation

   d. Exhalation

94. The movement of waste gases from the alveoli into the atmosphere is_____?

   a. Inspiration

   b. Expiration

   c. Inhalation

   d. Exhalation

95. _____ occurs when an individual is unable to move an adequate amount of air into the lungs using the diaphragm and intercostal muscles to meet the body's needs?

   a. Upper respiration infection

   b. Lower respiratory infection

   c. Respiratory distress

   d. None of the above

96. Which of the following is not a upper respiratory track infection?
    a. Common cold
    b. Sinusitis
    c. Pneumonia
    d. Allergy Rhinitis

97. _____ occurs when the muscles in the posterior pharynx that supports the soft palate, uvula, tonsils and tongues relax during sleep?
    a. Pneumoconiosis
    b. Asthma
    c. Obstructive sleep apnea
    d. Lung cancer

98. Which of the following is a pulmonary system tumor?
    a. Pneumoconiosis
    b. Asthma
    c. Obstructive sleep apnea
    d. Lung cancer

99. _____ is a tough membrane that connects the heart to the diaphragm and serves as a physical barrier to protect the heart again infection from the lungs?

a. Parietal pericardium

b. Visceral pericardium

c. Pericardial cavity

d. Pericardial fluid

100. The chamber of the heart that pumps the blood out is called?

a. Atria

b. Ventricles

c. Venae cavae

d. Pulmonary artery

101. The middle layer of the heart is the?

a. Epicardium

b. Myocardium

c. Endocardium

d. Pericardium

102. The chamber of the heart that receives blood is called?

a. Atria

b. Ventricles

c. Venae cavae

d. Pulmonary artery

103. The cardiac impulse originates in specialized tissue called the?

a. Atrioventricular (AV) node

b. Sinoatrial (SA) node

c. Depolarization

d. Repolarization

104. Contraction of the atria and the ventricles is called?
   a. Atrioventricular (AV) node
   b. Sinoatrial (SA) node
   c. Depolarization
   d. Repolarization

105. After the chamber contracts, a period of electric recovery occurs called?
   a. Atrioventricular (AV) node
   b. Sinoatrial (SA) node
   c. Depolarization
   d. Repolarization

106. _____ is diagnosed if the patient's blood pressure is persistently higher than 119mm Hg systolic and/or 79mm Hg diastolic?
   a. Secondary hypertension
   b. Primary hypertension
   c. Purkinje fibers
   d. Chordae tendineae

107.   From the bundle branches, the transmission of the cardiac waves continues through a mass of cardiac muscle fibers known as?
   a. Secondary hypertension
   b. Primary hypertension
   c. Purkinje fibers
   d. Chordae tendineae

108.   _____ occurs because of a disease process in another body system, such as a renal disease or endocrine disorder?
   a. Secondary hypertension
   b. Primary hypertension
   c. Purkinje fibers
   d. Chordae tendineae

109.   Tendons that anchor the cusps of the heart valve to the papillary muscles of the myocardium, preventing valvular prolapse is?
   a. Secondary hypertension
   b. Primary hypertension
   c. Purkinje fibers
   d. Chordae tendineae

110.   Recurring cramping in the valve caused by poor circulation of blood to the muscles of the lower leg is?
   a. Intermittent claudication
   b. Scleroderma
   c. Marfan syndrome
   d. Bruit

111.   Abnormal sound or murmur heard on auscultation of an organ, vessel or gland is?
   a. Intermittent claudication
   b. Scleroderma
   c. Marfan syndrome
   d. Bruit

112.   An inherited condition characterized by elongation of the bones, joint hypermobility, abnormalities of the eyes and development of aortic aneurysm is?
   a. Intermittent claudication
   b. Scleroderma
   c. Marfan syndrome
   d. Bruit

113.   Autoimmune disorder that affects the blood vessels and connective tissue, causing fibrous degeneration of the major organs is?

a. Intermittent claudication
b. Scleroderma
c. Marfan syndrome
d. Bruit

114.   The left side heart failure usually results from?
a. Hypetension
b. Lung-disease
c. Vein disorder
d. Pulmonale

115.   Right side heart failure that occurs because of pulmonary hypertension associated with chronic obstructive pulmonary disease is called?
a. Hypetension
b. Lung-disease
c. Vein disorder
d. Pulmonale

116.   Inflammation of the outer layer of the heart causing reduced cardiac activity and pericardial effusion is?
a. Endocarditis
b. Myocarditis
c. Pericarditis

d. Orthostatic hypertension

117. _____ is diagnosed if the patient experiences a drop in blood pressure when standing, especially when quickly going from a prone or seated position to an upright one?
    a. Endocarditis
    b. Myocarditis
    c. Pericarditis
    d. Orthostatic hypertension

118. _____ carries deoxygenated blood from the right ventricle to the lungs and oxygenated blood back to the left atrium?
    a. Capillaries
    b. Arteries
    c. Veins
    d. Pulmonary system

119. _____ are a single epithelial cell thick so that nutrient and gases can cross through the wall to be exchanged on the cellular level?
    a. Capillaries
    b. Arteries
    c. Veins

d. Pulmonary system

120.　　The walls of the veins are thinner than those of the arteries because they do not contain a muscular lining?
    a. True
    b. False
    c. At times
    d. None of the above

121.　　If the medical assistant identifies a patient in shock he/she should?
    a. Check the patient regularly
    b. Wait for the first indicators to worse
    c. Start emergency treatment
    d. None of the above

122.　　Excessive loss of blood or body fluid is?
    a. Hypovolemic
    b. Septic
    c. Anaphylactic
    d. Cardiogenic

123.　　Systematic vasodilation caused by the release of bacterial endotoxins is?
    a. Hypovolemic
    b. Septic

c. Anaphylactic

d. Cardiogenic

124.   Systemic hypersensitivity to an allergen causing respiratory distress and vascular collapse is?

a. Hypovolemic

b. Septic

c. Anaphylactic

d. Cardiogenic

125.   If a thrombus becomes dislodged and begins to circulate through the general circulation, it is then called?

a. Embolus

b. Phlebitis

c. Deep vein thrombosis

d. Venography

126.   A thrombus with inflammatory changes that has attached to the deep venous system of the lower leg, causing a partial or complete obstruction of the vessel is?

a. Embolus

b. Phlebitis

c. Deep vein thrombosis

d. Venography

127. _____ is an inflammation of the vein most commonly seen in the lower leg?
   a. Embolus
   b. Phlebitis
   c. Deep vein thrombosis
   d. Venography

128. Which of the following is not an arterial disorder?
   a. Aneurysm
   b. Arteriosclerosis
   c. Rheumatism
   d. Atherosclerosis

129. Loss of fluid within the neurons and the shrinkage of dendrites causes the brain to get smaller at approximately age 50 years and continues to do so as we age?
   a. True
   b. False
   c. At times
   d. None of the above

130. The following are some of the reasons why aging persons are at greater risk for falling except?
   a. Sensorimotor changes in mobility

b. Osteoporosis

c. Cerebrovascular accident

d. None of the above

131. _____ occurs as a result of blockage to the outflow of aqueous humor, which causes an increase in intraocular pressure and damage to the optic nerve?

a. Cataracts

b. Glaucoma

c. Macular degeneration

d. None of the above

132. _____ are cloudy or opaque areas in the lens that causes blurring of vision; ring or halos around lights and objects; and a blue or yellow tint to the visual field?

a. Cataracts

b. Glaucoma

c. Macular degeneration

d. None of the above

133. As a medical assistant caring for an older patient who seems to be taking more time than scheduled you should?

a. Hurry them so that schedule can be maintained

b. Give them whatever time needed to prepare for examination

c. Reschedule them for another day

d. None of the above

134.   The following are changes caused by aging in each of the body systems except?

a. Sharp decline in estrogen for women

b. Decrease elasticity of lung tissue

c. Increase in muscle mass

d. Weakening of bladder muscle

135.   Which of the following is not a major disease or disorder faced by older patients?

a. Integumentary system changes

b. Increase risk of injury from falls

c. Sleep disorder

d. None of the above

136.   The secretion or discharge of tears is called?

a. Lamination

b. Lamenting

c. Lacrimation

d. Tearing

137. The essential part of elastic connective tissue that, when moist, is flexible and elastic is?
    a. Elastin
    b. Elasticity
    c. Collagen
    d. Costal

138. Protein that forms the inelastic fibers of tendons, ligaments and fascia is?
    a. Elastin
    b. Elasticity
    c. Collagen
    d. Costal

139. The relaxation phase of the heart during which chambers are refilling with blood is?
    a. AV node
    b. SA node
    c. Diastole
    d. Systole

140. When both the atria and ventricles contract and empty of blood is?
    a. AV node
    b. SA node
    c. Diastole

d. Systole

141.   This electrode is place on the 4th intercostals space, left of the sternum?
     a. V1
     b. V4
     c. V2
     d. V5

142.   This electrode is place on the 5th intercostals space, left midclavicular line?
     a. V1
     b. V4
     c. V2
     d. V5

143.   Part of the cardiac conduction system located between the atria and the ventricles is called?
     a. AV node
     b. SA node
     c. Myocardium
     d. Infarction

144.   Pacemaker of the heart, located in the right atrium is?
     a. AV node
     b. SA node

c. Myocardium

d. Infarction

145.   Which of the following is pertaining to the heart muscles?

a. AV node

b. SA node

c. Myocardial

d. Infarction

146.   Area of tissue that has died from lack of blood supply is called?

a. AV node

b. SA node

c. Myocardial

d. Infarction

147.   Specialized muscle fibers that conduct electrical impulses from AV node to ventricular myocardium?

a. Ischemic

b. Ectopic

c. Bundle of His

d. Bifurcates

148.   Machine used to deliver an electroshock to the heart through electrodes placed on the chest wall is?

a. Cardioversion
b. Defibrillator
c. Ectopic
d. None of the above

149.   Use of electroshock to convert an abnormal cardiac rhythm to a normal one is?

a. Cardioversion
b. Defibrillator
c. Ectopic
d. None of the above

150.   Which of the following is characterized by temporary interruption in the blood supply to a tissue or an organ?

a. Ischemic
b. Ectopic
c. Bundle of His
d. Bifurcates

151.   If the sinus rate goes beyond 100 per minute it is called?

a. Sinus Bradycardia
b. Sinus Cardia
c. Sinus Tachycardia

d. Arrhythmia

152. If the sinus rate goes below 60 per minute it is called?
   a. Sinus Bradycardia
   b. Sinus Cardia
   c. Sinus Tachycardia
   d. Arrhythmia

153. An irregular cardiac rhythm is called?
   a. Sinus Bradycardia
   b. Sinus Cardia
   c. Sinus Tachycardia
   d. Arrhythmia

154. _____is the first deflection from the baseline, it is typically smooth and rounded and should occur before each QRS complex?
   a. P wave
   b. QRS wave
   c. T wave
   d. Q wave

155. The return to baseline after atrial contraction is called?
   a. PR segment

b. PR interval

c. ST segment

d. QRS wave

156.   The time from the beginning of atrial contraction to the beginning of ventricular contraction is?

a. PR segment

b. PR interval

c. ST segment

d. QRS wave

157.   _____ reflects the time between the end of ventricular contraction and the beginning of ventricular recovery?

a. PR segment

b. PR interval

c. ST segment

d. QRS wave

158.   The standard ECG consist of 12 separate leads; the first three leads are called?

a. Precordial leads

b. Augmented lead

c. Regular lead

d. Standard lead

159.   The second three leads are called?

a. Precordial leads

b. Augmented lead

c. Regular lead

d. Standard lead

160.   Which of the following is not a type of lead?

a. Precordial leads

b. Augmented lead

c. Regular lead

d. Standard lead

161.   Which of the following is also called bipolar lead?

a. Precordial leads

b. Augmented lead

c. Regular lead

d. Standard lead

162.   When applying leads to the patient making the proper connections is facilitated by specific lead markings or color-coding on the end of each lead wire, the right leg is _____ color?

a. Red

b. Yellow

c. Green

d. White

163.   The left leg is marked by what color?
   a. Red
   b. Yellow
   c. Green
   d. White

164.   The right arm is marked by what color?
   a. Red
   b. Yellow
   c. Green
   d. White

165.   The "V2" is marked by what color?
   a. Red
   b. Yellow
   c. Green
   d. White

166.   The "V1" is marked by what color?
   a. Red
   b. Yellow
   c. Green
   d. White

167.   Which of the following is not an Artifact?
   a. Wandering baseline

b. Interrupted baseline

c. Disarranged baseline

d. Somatic tremor

168. _____ occurs when the stylus gradually shifts away from the center of the paper, usually resulting from slight movement of the patient during tracing or poor electrode attachment?

    a. Wandering baseline

    b. Interrupted baseline

    c. Disarranged baseline

    d. Somatic tremor

169. _____ occurs when the ventricles contract before they should for the next cardiac cycle?

    a. Premature atrial contraction

    b. Premature sinus rhythm

    c. Premature ventricular contraction

    d. Atrial arrhythmias

170. _____ occurs when the atria contract before they should for the next cardiac cycle?

    a. Premature atrial contraction

    b. Premature sinus rhythm

    c. Premature ventricular contraction

d. Atrial arrhythmias

171. _____ is conducted to observe and record the patient's cardiovascular response to measured exercise challenges?
   a. Cancer testing
   b. Stress testing
   c. Heart test
   d. None of the above

172. When conducting a stress test, the following are indications to terminate the test except?
   a. Patient is unable to continue
   b. When the patient is old
   c. When abnormalities appears on the monitor
   d. None of the above

173. An x-ray image is referred to as?
   a. Radiopaque
   b. Radiolucent
   c. Radiograph
   d. Radiation field

174. Substance that is easily penetrated by x-ray is called?

a. Radiopaque
b. Radiolucent
c. Radiograph
d. Radiation field

175.   The cross section of the x-ray beam at the point of use is called?
    a. Radiopaque
    b. Radiolucent
    c. Radiograph
    d. Radiation field

176.   Substance that is not easily penetrated by x-ray is called?
    a. Radiopaque
    b. Radiolucent
    c. Radiograph
    d. Radiation field

177.   Which of the following is not a prime factor of exposure?
    a. Exposure time
    b. Kilovoltage
    c. Light distance
    d. Milliamperage

178. _____ is a view of the body in which the individual is standing, facing the observer, with the palms of the hand forward?

  a. Anatomic position
  b. Sagittal plane
  c. Coronal plane
  d. Tranverse plane

179. The _____ divides the body into anterior and posterior parts?

  a. Anatomic position
  b. Sagittal plane
  c. Coronal plane
  d. Tranverse plane

180. The _____ divides the body into superior and inferior positions?

  a. Anatomic position
  b. Sagittal plane
  c. Coronal plane
  d. Tranverse plane

181. What does this x-ray positions "prone" mean?

  a. Lying down
  b. Lying face down
  c. Lying on the back face up
  d. Seated

182. What does this x-ray positions "upright" mean?
   a. Lying down
   b. Lying face down
   c. Lying on the back face up
   d. Seated

183. What does this x-ray positions "Supine" mean?
   a. Lying down
   b. Lying face down
   c. Lying on the back face up
   d. Seated

184. The term "plantar" describes which location on/within the body?
   a. Sole of the foot
   b. Towards the head
   c. Towards the tail or end of the body
   d. Side

185. The term "Cephalic" describes which location on/within the body?
   a. Sole of the foot
   b. Towards the head
   c. Towards the tail or end of the body

d. Side

186.   The term "Caudal" describes which
location on/within the body?
    a. Sole of the foot
    b. Towards the head
    c. Towards the tail or end of the body
    d. Side

187.   All patients who are allergic to shellfish
will also be allergic to iodine dye?
    a. True
    b. False
    c. At times
    d. None of the above

188.   _____ is a noninvasive diagnostic
modality that allows visualization of anatomic
structures without the use of radioactive x-
rays?
    a. Sonography
    b. Nuclear medicine images
    c. Magnetic resonance imaging (MRI)
    d. None of the above

189.   _____ is created by scanning the
patient after special radioactive materials

called tracers have been swallowed or injected intravenously?
   a. Sonography
   b. Nuclear medicine images
   c. Magnetic resonance imaging (MRI)
   d. None of the above

190.   Interventional technique using a catheter to open or widen a blood vessel to improve circulation is?
   a. Angiography
   b. Angioplasty
   c. Angiocardiography
   d. Arteriography

191.   Radiography of the heart and great vessels using an iodine contrast medium is?
   a. Angiography
   b. Angioplasty
   c. Angiocardiography
   d. Arteriography

192.   Radiography of blood vessel using an iodine contrast medium is?
   a. Angiography
   b. Angioplasty
   c. Angiocardiography

d. Arteriography

193. Fluoroscopic examination of the soft tissue components of joints with direct injection of a contrast medium into the joint capsule is?
   a. Axial projection
   b. Arthrogram
   c. Aortogram
   d. Fluoroscopy

194. Radiographic examination of the urinary tract using intravenous injection of an iodine medium is?
   a. Intravenous urogram
   b. Intravenography
   c. Tracers
   d. Roentgen

195. Radioactive substances administered to patients for nuclear medicine imaging procedures is?
   a. Intravenous urogram
   b. Intravenography
   c. Tracers
   d. Transducer

196. Fluoroscopic examination of the colon, usually employing rectal administration of barium sulfate as a contrast medium is?
   a. Upper gastrointestinal series
   b. Lower gastrointestinal series
   c. Phosphor
   d. Mid-gastrointestinal series

197. Fluoroscopic examination of the esophagus, stomach and duodenum using oral administration of barium sulfate as a contrast medium is?
   a. Upper gastrointestinal series
   b. Lower gastrointestinal series
   c. Phosphor
   d. Mid-gastrointestinal series

198. "NPO" means?
   a. No position offered
   b. Never prescribe this medication
   c. New patient out
   d. Nothing by mouth

199. Part of the sonography machine that is in contact with the patient; and sends high frequency sound waves and receives the sound

echoes that return from the patient's body is called?

    a. Intravenous urogram

    b. Intravenography

    c. Tracers

    d. Transducer

200.   Plane that divides the body into right and left part is called?

    a. Oblique projection

    b. Sagittal plane

    c. Coronal plane

    d. Tranverse plane

201.   _____ is the most effective way of preventing infection

    a. Hand washing

    b. Regular doctor visits

    c. Immunization

    d. Keeping away from people with infection

202.   The medical assistant is responsible for the following except?

    a. Collecting specimen

    b. Instructing patient

    c. Request laboratory testing for a patient

d. Performing CLIA-testing

203.   A sac filled with blood that may be the result of trauma is called?
   a. Hemolyzed
   b. Hematoma
   c. Specimen
   d. Anticoagulants

204.   A sample of body fluid, waste product, or tissue that is collected for analysis is?
   a. Hemolyzed
   b. Hematoma
   c. Specimen
   d. Anticoagulants

205.   A term used to describe a blood sample in which the red blood cells have ruptured?
   a. Hemolyzed
   b. Hematoma
   c. Specimen
   d. Anticoagulants

206.   Chemicals added to the blood after collection to prevent clotting is?
   a. Hemolyzed
   b. Hematoma

c. Specimen

d. Anticoagulants

207.   Cylindric glass or plastic tubes used to deliver fluids is?

   a. Cylinder

   b. Fluid tubes

   c. Plastic bottles

   d. Pipets

208.   _____ is known to cause birth defects?

   a. Teratogenic

   b. Cytology

   c. Cerebrospinal fluid

   d. Carcinogen

209.   _____ are materials or situations that present a risk or potential risk of infection?

   a. Physical hazard

   b. Chemical hazard

   c. Biologic hazard

   d. None of the above

210.   In the hazard identification system developed by the National Fire Protection Association, the top diamond shape is?

   a. Red

b. White

c. Yellow

d. Blue

211. The top diamond shape indicates?
   a. Hazard to health
   b. Flammability hazard
   c. Reactive or stability hazard
   d. Radioactivity, special biohazard/dangerous situations

212. In the hazard identification system developed by the National Fire Protection Association, the diamond shape on the left is?
   a. Red
   b. White
   c. Yellow
   d. Blue

213. The diamond shape on the left indicates?
   a. Hazard to health
   b. Flammability hazard
   c. Reactive or stability hazard
   d. Radioactivity, special biohazard/dangerous situations

214.   In the hazard identification system developed by the National Fire Protection Association, the bottom diamond shape is?
    a. Red
    b. White
    c. Yellow
    d. Blue

215.   The bottom diamond shape indicates?
    a. Hazard to health
    b. Flammability hazard
    c. Reactive or stability hazard
    d. Radioactivity,   special biohazard/dangerous situations

216.   In the hazard identification system developed by the National Fire Protection Association, the diamond shape on the right is?
    a. Red
    b. White
    c. Yellow
    d. Blue

217.   The diamond shape on the right indicates?
    a. Hazard to health
    b. Flammability hazard

c. Reactive or stability hazard

d. Radioactivity,   special biohazard/dangerous situations

218.   Which of the following is not an essential element of a laboratory requisition?

a. Test ordered

b. Time the specimen was collected

c. Age of patient

d. Ordering physician

219.   _____ involves procedures undertaken to ensure that each patient is provided excellent care?

a. Quality assurance

b. Management control

c. Quality assurance

d. Total quality management

220.   _____ is ensuring that laboratory testing is accurate and reliable?

a. Quality assurance

b. Management control

c. Quality control

d. Total quality management

221.   The most important requirement for a collection container is that it should be?

a. Plastic

b. White

c. Clean

d. Disposable

222. _____ is the most commonly analyzed body fluid in the clinical laboratory?

a. Sweat

b. Urine

c. Stool

d. Blood

223. Which of the following is not a component of the physical examination of urine?

a. Odor

b. Blood

c. Color

d. Turbidity

224. Which of the following is not a component of the chemical examination of urine?

a. Protein

b. Ketones

c. Leukocyte

d. Foam

225. Which of these is not a formed element found in urine sediment?
   a. Casts
   b. Cells
   c. Crystals
   d. None of the above

226. The following are means in which urine could be adulterated before drug testing except?
   a. Consuming excess water before urinating
   b. Adding water to a urine specimen
   c. Performing a clean catch of urine
   d. Adding chemicals to adulterate urine

227. Voided means?
   a. Invalid
   b. Cancelled
   c. Urinated
   d. Not accepted

228. Tubular structures found in urine composed mainly of mucoprotein secreted by certain cells of the kidney is called?
   a. Casts
   b. Cystoscopy

c. Crystals

d. Filtrate

229. A telescopic examination of the urinary bladder is called?

 a. Casts

 b. Cystoscopy

 c. Crystals

 d. Filtrate

230. Essential amino acid found in milk, egg and other foods is?

 a. Supravital

 b. Phenylalanine

 c. Myoglobinuria

 d. Glycosuria

231. Presence of glucose in the urine is called?

 a. Supravital

 b. Phenylalanine

 c. Myoglobinuria

 d. Glycosuria

232. Abnormal presence of a hemoglobin-like chemical of muscle tissue in urine that is the result of muscle deterioration is?
   a. Supravital
   b. Phenylalanine
   c. Myoglobinuria
   d. Glycosuria

233. Medical assistant trained to perform phlebotomy are certified and licensed phlebotomist?
   a. True
   b. False
   c. At times
   d. None of the above

234. _____ are used on small veins such as those in the hand or in pediatric patients?
   a. Syringe
   b. Butterfly needles
   c. Multisample needles
   d. All of the above

235. _____ are commonly used in routine adult venipuncture, when several tubes are to be drawn during a single venipuncture?

a. Syringe

b. Butterfly needles

c. Multisample needles

d. All of the above

236. When collecting a blood sample which of the following should be removed first?

a. Needle

b. Tourniquet

c. Gloves

d. Any of the above

237. The following are equipment needed for venipuncture for children except?

a. Tourniquet

b. Alcohol

c. Toy to keep children still

d. Latex gloves

238. Which of the following is used to prevent venous flow out of the site, making veins easier to locate and puncture?

a. Sterile bandage

b. Tourniquet

c. gauze

d. pad

239. The tourniquet should not be left on for more than _____minute(s) in order to prevent hemoconcentration, from the time blood flow begins
   a. one
   b. three
   c. five
   d. ten

240. Discard needle into the:
   a. biohazards sharp container
   b. Polythene bag
   c. Leather bag
   d. Trash bin

241. _____ is a measurement of the percentage of packed RBCs in a volume of blood?
   a. RBC testing
   b. Hematocrit
   c. Blood count
   d. None of the above

242. Which of the following is not a main function of blood?
   a. Supplies cells with needed nutrient
   b. Delivers oxygen to tissue
   c. Removes waste
   d. None of the above

243. Which of these cells is responsible for antibody production?
   a. "T" cells
   b. "C" cells
   c. "B" cells
   d. "R" cells

244. Which of the following is also called "kissing disease"?
   a. Helicobacter pylori
   b. Lyme disease
   c. Infectious mononucleosis
   d. Fungi

245. An infection not present before admittance to the hospital but originated in the hospital is called?
   a. Nosocomial
   b. Organelles
   c. Microorganism
   d. Prokaryote

246. The act of scraping a body cavity with surgical instrument is called?
   a. Dilatation
   b. Curettage
   c. Patency

d. Dissect

247. Open condition of a body cavity or canal is?
   a. Dilatation
   b. Curettage
   c. Patency
   d. Dissect

248. The following are expectations that employers expects from their medical assistant employee except?
   a. Good Appearance
   b. Dependability
   c. Dressing
   d. Job skills

249. Which of the following is an error to be avoided on a resume?
   a. Skills
   b. Accomplishment
   c. Photograph
   d. Summary of experience

250. Which of the following is unnecessary on a resume?
   a. Email address

b. Number of years of previous experience
c. Salary expectation
d. Career objectives

MA Test 4	
1	C
2	B
3	C
4	A
5	B
6	C
7	D
8	C
9	B
10	D
11	C
12	D
13	A
14	A
15	A
16	D
17	A
18	D
19	B
20	C
21	D
22	A
23	B
24	C
25	B
26	A
27	B

28	C
29	A
30	C
31	C
32	B
33	D
34	C
35	A
36	B
37	D
38	C
39	A
40	C
41	B
42	A
43	D
44	C
45	A
46	B
47	D
48	C
49	B
50	A
51	D
52	C
53	C
54	A
55	A
56	B
57	B
58	D
59	C

60	A
61	B
62	A
63	D
64	B
65	B
66	D
67	D
68	B
69	B
70	A
71	B
72	C
73	C
74	D
75	B
76	C
77	D
78	A
79	B
80	C
81	B
82	A
83	A
84	B
85	A
86	B
87	B
88	A
89	D
90	A
91	D

92	D
93	A
94	B
95	C
96	C
97	C
98	D
99	A
100	B
101	B
102	A
103	B
104	C
105	D
106	B
107	C
108	A
109	D
110	A
111	D
112	C
113	B
114	A
115	D
116	C
117	D
118	D
119	A
120	A
121	C
122	A
123	B

124	C
125	A
126	C
127	B
128	C
129	A
130	D
131	B
132	A
133	B
134	C
135	D
136	C
137	A
138	C
139	C
140	D
141	C
142	B
143	A
144	B
145	C
146	D
147	C
148	B
149	A
150	A
151	C
152	A
153	D
154	A
155	A

156	B
157	C
158	D
159	B
160	C
161	D
162	C
163	A
164	D
165	B
166	A
167	C
168	A
169	C
170	A
171	B
172	B
173	C
174	B
175	D
176	A
177	C
178	A
179	C
180	D
181	B
182	D
183	C
184	A
185	B
186	C
187	A

188	C
189	B
190	B
191	C
192	A
193	B
194	A
195	C
196	B
197	A
198	D
199	D
200	B
201	A
202	C
203	B
204	C
205	A
206	D
207	D
208	A
209	C
210	A
211	B
212	D
213	A
214	B
215	D
216	C
217	C
218	C
219	A

220	C
221	C
222	B
223	B
224	D
225	D
226	C
227	C
228	A
229	B
230	B
231	D
232	C
233	B
234	B
235	C
236	B
237	C
238	B
239	A
240	A
241	B
242	D
243	C
244	C
245	A
246	B
247	C
248	C
249	C
250	C